Organizational Change through Lean Methodologies

Organizational Change through Lean Methodologies

A Guide for Successful Implementation

A. Heri Iswanto

Routledge
Taylor & Francis Group

A PRODUCTIVITY PRESS BOOK

First published 2021
by Routledge
600 Broken Sound Parkway #300, Boca Raton, FL, 33487

and by Routledge
2 Park Square, Milton Park, Abingdon, Oxon, OX14 4RN

Routledge is an imprint of the Taylor & Francis Group, an informa business

© 2021 Taylor & Francis

The right of A. Heri Iswanto to be identified as author of this work has been asserted by him in accordance with sections 77 and 78 of the Copyright, Designs and Patents Act 1988.

Library of Congress Control Number: 2020941560

ISBN: 9780367488826 (hbk)
ISBN: 9780367488819 (pbk)
ISBN: 9781003043324 (ebk)

Typeset in Garamond
by codeMantra

To my loving wife, Shika,
and our children, Naya and Farrel

Contents

Acknowledgments

I want to praise the Almighty, Allah SWT, for the mercy and blessings I've been given so I could complete this book, *Organizational Change through Lean Methodologies: A Guide for Successful Implementation.*

I extend special thanks to my colleagues, who always give me motivation; my beloved wife, Shika Iswanto, who always supports me; and my dears, Kannaya and Alfarrel, who have been waiting patiently and gave their time until the completion of this book.

I realize that this book is still far from being perfect. However, I have performed my best in presenting it. Therefore, suggestions and criticism are always welcome for betterment. Finally, I hope that the book is useful for professionals, practitioners, academics in general, and especially those who want to conduct similar research about Lean.

Author

A. Heri Iswanto completed his Doctorate of Economic Science majoring in Sustainable Development Management at Trisakti International Business School in the University of Trisakti, affiliated with Colorado State University (USA). He completed his Master's and Bachelor's degrees in Hospital Management in the Faculty of Public Health, University of Indonesia.

He works as an associate professor at Public Health in the Faculty of Health Science, University of Pembangunan National Veteran Jakarta, and as a lecturer at other universities in Jakarta. He has been the Senator Secretary of University, Vice Dean, and Dean of Faculty of Health Science.

He has also been director at various hospitals including Prikasih, Lestari, Kemang Medical Care, Budhi Jaya, and Ali Sibroh Malisi. He was an active speaker in many national and international conferences and has conducted trainings in the United States, Taiwan (Republic of China), IR Iran, Pakistan, Thailand, Malaysia, Singapore, Japan, Tiongkok/China, the Philippines, and Vietnam.

Chapter 1

What is Lean?

Lean is a type of organizational change brought through improvement methods based on a cost reduction mechanism. It is based on the assumption that by reducing costs, organizations can work better (Achanga, Shehab, Roy, & Nelder, 2006). All changes in lean-based organizations are directed at reducing the costs. Cost reduction will increase efficiency since, basically, it removes process inefficiencies and decreases cycle time (Näslund, 2008).

Why are targets directed at cost reduction? Because costs are a crucial factor for sustainable business organizations (Achanga et al., 2006). The sustainability of an organization can be achieved by either internal method of cost reduction or external method by getting as many customers as possible. External method is more difficult than internal method because the external world has a greater uncertainty than the internal world. In the internal environment, we know how the process occurs and what happens in a running process. However, these factors cannot be perfectly tracked in an external environment. There are so many factors that rise and fall in the external world. It is certainly better if some efforts to achieve sustainability are made by balancing internal and external aspects. However, let the internal aspects are under the management of marketing team. So, lean will only focus on the internal aspects of cost reduction.

Nevertheless, the external world has an effect on the internal environment. The customers, government, the wider community, trading partners, business competitors, all affect costs in many ways. Customers demand a more representative price with good quality, so the company must add costs to pursue quality, which ultimately reduces profits. The government poses limits on the price and production practices that often require additional investment to be in line with the government regulation. The societies and Non Government Organization (NGO) pay attention to company's compliance with the government and community needs. Trading partners, for example, suppliers, also pose price limits. The competitors will issue more affordable products with the same quality if the company is making too much profit.

The rapidly changing contemporary environment with new inventions and lifestyles makes the problem of cost reduction more complex than before, not to mention the sustainability of the organization. If the organization manages to survive, it will grow bigger; receive more customers; operate in more countries; deal with more suppliers, competitors; and so on. Lean is directed at the efforts to deal with the problem of cost reduction in this rapidly changing contemporary environment. Lean has gained a status of being the most effective business improvement technique so far (Näslund, 2008).

So, what is lean actually? Womack and Jones define lean as "a systematic elimination of waste by all organization members from all fields of value stream". Value stream is "all activities needed to manufacture products" (Näslund, 2008). It is defined as value stream because these activities reflect a flowing stream from the input to the expected product output. This stream is certainly not as simple as a river's flow. Value stream has a number of interacting fields. Some of the steps in these fields may be inefficient, so they are wasteful. Lean removes this waste systematically by involving all organization members.

Another definition is proposed by Kilpatrick. According to Kilpatrick, lean is "a systematic approach to identify and remove waste through continuous improvement that flowing products based on customer attraction to pursue perfection" (Sunder, 2013). This definition is more complex. He also includes the identification of waste as a lean form. It means that lean starts as soon as the waste is identified. This is different from Womack and Jones's definition stating that lean starts from a waste removal process. This definition does not contain the implementation component by all organization members, but the concept of value stream remains. The value stream is indicated in the term "flowing the product". Furthermore, this definition mentions how to identify and eliminate these wastes by continuous improvement based on the customer's attraction. Identifying and eliminating unsustainable waste or based on encouragement from the company, rather than attraction from the customer, does not include lean. This definition also emphasizes lean goals. The aim of lean is to pursue perfection. Perfection here is 100% efficiency. This perfection causes lean to be sustainable. In addition, 100% efficiency cannot be achieved instantly. It requires an iterative process, which is continuously improving on the details; thus, even the smallest waste is finally eliminated.

Actually, Womack has another broader definition of lean. It says, "an approach which requires a commitment of technical, social, and human capital from an organization to conduct continuous improvement, with the purpose of identifying different ways to create value as determined by customers and eliminate waste based on in-depth examination of root causes" (Flumerfelt & Green, 2013). This definition was proposed earlier than Kilpatrick's. It has a sustainability concern by asserting that lean is conducted continuously. It has also considered the problem of attraction from customers by stating that it is determined by the customers. This definition does not talk about systematic approach, identification of waste, or value stream. However, this definition adds some new points. In this definition, lean requires not only commitment from all organization members but also technical and social commitment. He also adds that lean does not only facilitate the value stream but also creates new values. Indeed, new values can also be interpreted as values arising due to value stream efficiency. It is a covered old value and seen when inefficiencies are removed. This definition is also more practical. He emphasizes how waste is removed by examining deeply the root causes of waste.

Lean has more definitions among the practitioners, educators, and thinkers (Martichenko & Taylor, 2006). Here are the five definitions given by Martichenko and Taylor (2006):

1. Lean is an organizational methodology designed to create a learning organization through the culture of focusing on problem-solving and continuous cooperation.
2. Lean is a philosophy based on the reduction of lead time from customer orders to product/service delivery.
3. Lean is a manufacturing method based on production which relies on customer's demand and focuses on one-piece flow.
4. Lean is an operational model that cuts economic value of scale and focuses on cost reduction as a result of small incremental improvements continuously.
5. Lean is a set of tools to reduce waste, where waste is defined as processes that do not add value.

Let us have a look at these definitions of lean one by one. The first definition is highlighting the effects of lean. However, since lean process works by leading to continuous improvement, it will certainly have an impact on the organization habits. It is a learning habit as it produces improvement from identification and roots of waste. These habits will in turn be deeply rooted as the lean effort becomes a learning culture. Furthermore, because this learning culture is at the organizational level, it can be said that it produces learning organization. As a result, it can be said that lean creates a learning organization.

Is lean then said to aim at creating a learning organization? It could be, if we look at it from a long-term perspective. Cost reduction is a short-term perspective and often criticized for creating a superficial thought and less exploiting lean. If we want to truly obtain the greatest benefits of lean, we must raise it to a broader level, which is the organizational changes toward learning organization. After all, not all organizations are oriented to costs and business profits. Non-profit organizations or organizations with an unlimited supply of costs may not care about costs. Long-term options for creating learning organization are very promising offers of lean implementation.

The second definition, that lean is a philosophy based on the reduction of lead time, is a bit confusing. Philosophy is very deep and abstract, while lead time reduction is very practical and operational. This definition could have been more proper if it talked about the philosophy or lead time reduction only. If we raise philosophical issue, this can be relevant if there is a long-term target, rather than reducing the costs. The goal of transforming an organization into learning organization requires an in-depth, comprehensive, and strategic thinking, so that it will become feasible to use this philosophical concept as a foundation.

If we raise the lead time reduction issue, the result will be contradictory, as lean deals with time and cost reduction. Time reduction can increase the cost and vice versa. If time reduction is included as one of the lean goals, cost reduction must also be included. Otherwise, there is a dilemma and the problem will develop into an optimization problem, instead of management problem. Optimization means maximizing one side to the point that it can be tolerated by the other side. If optimization is directed at cost reduction, then optimization means an effort to minimize costs to the point where customers can tolerate extended time due to cost reduction. If optimization is directed at time reduction, then it is an attempt to minimize waiting time to the extent where the company can still tolerate the increasing costs due to the waiting time reduction. This point has been covered by the problem of eliminating waste or the concept of customer attraction. In further discussion, we will find that there are many types of wastes, including waste of time, money, and other wastes.

So, the second definition does not provide enough input for actual meaning of lean. The third definition introduces a new concept, the one-piece flow. However, this is actually a term that is closely related to customer attraction. One-piece flow means the flow of product when the customer demands it. It will minimize inventory which becomes a waste of its own. In fact, this definition also includes customer demand as the basis of lean. As a result, the third definition only talks about customer attraction.

The fourth definition addresses three points: cutting economic value of scale, focusing on cost reduction, and small incremental improvement in a continuous manner. Economic value of scale means that value increases as the amount of goods produced increases. This is an old-fashioned way of thinking that it is ignoring the aspects of efficiency. This mindset believes that to obtain profits, the amount of goods production should be improved. This is problematic, since sometimes, if the addition is an overload, the price will decrease. Consequently, the average profit per product also decreases. Even if the price does not fall, there will be a large stockpile because the number of buyers will be fewer than the goods sold. Lean cuts the economic value of scale by orienting not on how the biggest production is possible. In fact, in the concept of customer attraction, goods are only produced when customers exist. It means, there is no inventory at all. It is said to be almost nothing, not nothing at all, because the manufactured products are nearly 100% impossible to be the same as the number of customers' demand. Absolute equality only occurs in the industries that are producing their products by the customer request. Most of them are industries with a large production and a large number of dynamic customers, such as products sold in minimarkets.

Lean cuts the value of scale production by looking at the existing waste. Production remains the same, but the cost of goods production is lesser due to the loss of waste. As a result, companies do not have to increase their production if it is not required, yet the companies have gained an increase in average profits due to lean. It becomes the second part of the fourth definition which focuses on cost reduction. The focus on cost reduction can be included in the overall lean concept, since cost wasting is only a part of the existing waste. Actually, other wastes can be converted into costs or, in other words, perceived by the money value.

The third component of the fourth definition is a continuous, small incremental improvement. It has been discussed in the concept of continuous improvement. However, the term "small" in that definition is controversial. If major improvement is more profitable, why we have to make the small improvement. That is why the term "improvement" better captures the lean concept than the term "small improvement".

Then follows the fifth definition which sees lean as a set of tools to reduce waste. Waste is defined as a process that does not add value. This definition is quite precise and simple. Whether lean is a set of tools, philosophy, a systematic approach, or the like depends on the point of view. If we take a broad and general perspective, lean is a philosophy. If we look at it from a short-term perspective, it is a systematic approach. If we look at it from a very practical point of view, then it is a set of tools.

Let us have a look at other definitions. Wang et al. (2012) proposed the following definition: lean is "the pursuit of perfection by removing waste, aligning with the inclusion of practices that are contributing to the reduction of costs and schedules while improving the performance of product, process, and organization as a whole" (Wang, Ming, Kong, Li, & Wang, 2011). This definition addresses the ultimate goal, the pursuit of perfection. They talk about how lean is conducted, which is by removing waste and aligning with the inclusion of practices that are contributing to cost reduction and schedules. Costs and schedules are two short-term goals. Wang et al. compromised the view that lean must reduce costs or lean must reduce lead time. We have mentioned that time is only one form of waste among many other types of wastes. All types of wastes can be cashed in, so waste reduction can also mean cost reduction. Actually, cost reduction does not need to be included in the lean definition.

If we take a glance at the phrase "aligned with the inclusion of practices", it is actually unnecessary because these practices are form of waste reduction which has been mentioned at the beginning of the definition. However, there are some actions that are reducing costs and schedules without considering whether there is a waste or not. For instance, using new technology can be an instant practice that does not require waste identification. We only decide whether some activities such as purchasing information technology to eliminate written medical records, for instance, are lean or not. If we rely on the definition of waste as the things that do not add value, then the purchase of new technology is not a lean form. New technology only enhances things with added value so that it gives a higher value. However, if we rely on the definition of waste as the issue that is hindering value creation, we can include new technology or other practices that are reducing costs and schedules as part of the lean definition. New technology and related practices are those that are able to add and create new values for processes with value. We know that lean does not only remove things that do not provide value but it also creates new values. Therefore, we can take the second opinion, that "aligned with the inclusion of practices that is contributing to cost and schedule reduction", as part of lean.

From the above explanation, we can conclude the characteristics of lean as follows:

1. Lean is a philosophy, systematic approach, and set of tools.
2. Lean works by identifying and eliminating waste.
3. Waste elimination is conducted by aligning the inclusion of practices that add and create value.
4. Lean works based on the customer attraction.
5. Waste elimination is conducted through an in-depth examination of root cause of waste.
6. Lean is performed by all organization members and all technical and social capital.
7. Lean is held by collaboration and focus on the problem.
8. Lean is implemented in all fields of value stream.
9. Lean is implemented continuously.
10. Lean pursues perfection.
11. Lean creates organizational change into a learning organization.

To make it clearer, we can understand this issue by looking at the chart of causal relationship (Figure 1.1).

From the conceptual model and the limitation, we can define lean in a broad, narrow, and brief sense. The broad definition of lean is as follows:

> Lean is a systematic approach to identify waste, root cause of waste, waste elimination in all areas of value, and the inclusion of practices that add and create value based on the customer attraction by collaboration and focus of all organization members with their technical and social capital to achieve cost efficiency in a sustainable way to pursue perfection.

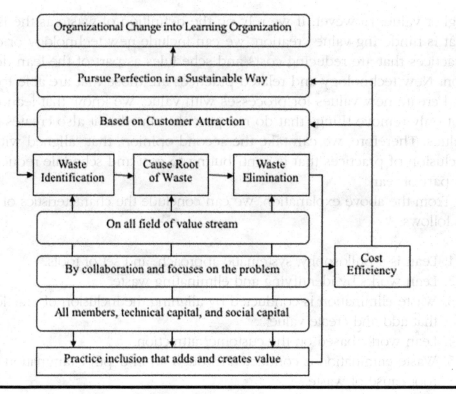

Figure 1.1   Lean conceptual model.

If this definition is shortened, we can draw three main characteristics to form a definition. The short definition is as follows:

> Lean is value creation for customer by minimizing waste.

At a more abstract level, we can define lean as follows:

> Lean is a philosophy leading to value creation for customers by minimizing waste so that it creates change in an organization to become a learning organization.

Chapter 2

History of Lean

Many people think that lean originated in Japan. However, the history of lean actually began in 1926. At that time, Henry Ford published his book *Today and Tomorrow*. Henry Ford was the owner of Ford, the affordable and most popular automotive brand in the United States. This book explains in detail the continuous improvement practices, including one-piece flow, just-in-time (JIT), and other lean tools. Henry Ford stated:

> One of the most noteworthy accomplishments in keeping the price of Ford products low is the gradual shortening of the production cycle. The longer an article is in the process of manufacture and the more it is moved about, the greater is its ultimate cost. (Kilpatrick, 2003)

Ford considered that a performance without mistakes can only be achieved through the identification of various waste sources in manufacturing process. Waste according to Ford is the use of human in the production process. Therefore, he strongly supported automation in manufacturing. In fact, Ford is known as the father of mass production (Alizon, Shooter, & Simpson, 2009). Ford stated in his book:

> The old way was to guess. We cannot afford to guess. We cannot afford to leave any process to human judgment. (D'Angelo & Zarbo, 2007)

Regarding quality, Ford defined quality as follows:

> Quality is doing it right when no one is looking. (Zarbo, 2012)

Ford's idea above was then called the Henry Ford Production System (HFPS) (Cankovic et al., 2009). HFPS produced a better T car model than the previous product. The T model produced in 1926 had more complete features such as headlight, windshield, more aerodynamic shapes, bumper, door, wire wheels, etc., compared with the previous generation in 1908 (Alizon et al., 2009). Now, HFPS is a term used by researchers working under Henry Ford Foundation group, including Henry Ford Hospital, to refer to the lean quality improvement model (Figure 2.1) (Cankovic et al., 2009).

After losing in World War II, Japan began to rise. Rather than importing cars from Ford and other suppliers, Japan began to produce their own

Figure 2.1 1908 and 1926 T models (Alizon et al., 2009).

cars. One of the Japanese automotive products is Toyota. In 1948, Sakichi Toyoda, owner of Toyota, contacted an engineer, Taiichi Ohno, asking him to develop a system to produce a high-quality vehicle efficiently. Toyoda's dream was more or less the same as Ford's. Furthermore, Taiichi Ohno collaborated with Shigeo Shingo and brother of Sakichi, Eiji Toyoda, to create the Toyota Production System (TPS) (Manning, 2011).

TPS relied on Henry Ford's principles. In fact, Ohno had conducted a study in Ford's manufacturing unit in Michigan, United States, with Sakichi and his son, Kiichiro Toyoda, in the 1950s. They were not impressed with the automation shown by the assembly and mass production lines at Ford factory. They even thought that some methods were less effective. There were still a lot of inventory piling up, the work was imbalanced in some division of the factory, and the final process was still loaded with a lot of re-work (Humphreys, 2011).

In fact, they were actually impressed by the vending machine in Piggly Wiggly supermarket. When the customers inserted their money to buy a drink, the machine would immediately dispense the drink and replaced the empty space by a can behind it. The same thing also happened on all supplies in the supermarket (Toyota Production System, 2009).

Back to Japan, they implemented this principle to an inventory system called JIT. This observation inspired Ohno and his colleagues only to stock up on one level as needed by their employees. As a result, inventory became minimum and the employees did not feel troubled (Toyota Production System, 2009).

TPS was created to get rid of excessive burden and inconsistency and remove waste in Toyota automotive manufacturing system. The main philosophy of TPS is called The Toyota Way. Basic philosophy of Toyota Way is "base your management decisions on a long-term philosophy, even at the expense of short-term financial goals" (Toyota Production System, 2009). TPS uses three types of concepts (Manning, 2011):

1. *Muri* is excessive load. The meaning of *muri* is not to overload equipment or employees. Muri directs employees to solve various problems that are burdening them. These problems include safety issues, ergonomic problems, searching for equipment, waiting for approval, waiting for assistance, and other heavy burdens for employees, customers, and equipment.
2. *Mura* is inconsistency, meaning the uniformity in flow. *Mura* emerges due to inefficient use of people, materials, or machines. Two solutions

to solve *mura* are the JIT system and the pull system. JIT focuses on providing products when the product is actually ordered. The pull system focuses on providing products at a quantity that is really needed for inventory. The term "pull" means when an item is needed, the item is pulled from the system. It requires recording and monitoring of inventory quantities and other efforts to avoid overproduction.

3. *Muda* means waste. *Muda* is the elimination of anything that do not give value to the product directly. *Muda* includes many issues, including issues in *muri* and *mura*. An example of *muda* is employee empowerment and avoiding queues for the decision of management. TPS formulates the seven types of waste, namely (Toyota Production System, 2009)

   1. Overproduction
   2. Transportation
   3. Waiting
   4. Motion
   5. Extra processing
   6. Inventory
   7. Defect (re-working and scrapping)

In 1975, TPS claimed to have succeeded in increasing the number of units of production per employee, almost 50 times more than in 1948 (Manning, 2011). In 2007, Toyota became the largest car company in the world with its profits equal to all car companies combined (Toyota Production System, 2009).

During 1950–1952, Dr. W. Edward Deming, father of quality, gave a series of lectures to groups of scientists and engineers who were the members of Japan Union of Scientists and Engineers (JUSE) as well as to entrepreneurs in Japan (Wawak, 2018). It was a part their effort to invite quality experts from the West to boost their product quality. At that time, Japanese used to export low-quality products. However, there was a high-quality culture in some companies, inherited from World War II. Juran (2003) observed that this happened due to the fact that all Japanese products were good in quality during the war to support their military in World War II.

During his studies in Japan, Deming gave a lecture on the Shewhart cycle. The Shewhart cycle was first developed by Walter Shewhart in the early 1930s to develop methodologies to improve industrial quality. Shewhart was a physicist who worked at Western Electric. This method relies on statistical processes control and scientific application in general. Shewhart put details of this development in his book, *Statistical Method from the Viewpoint of Quality Control*. He also wrote scientific papers related to measurement errors in 1934 in the *Reviews of Modern Physics*. One component in this method is the Shewhart cycle. The Shewhart cycle consisted of only three components, that is, specification, production, and inspection. Shewhart then developed more detailed tools to implement the cycle. For example, Shewhart developed the use of control graph in inspection activity. This graph allows the inspector to measure product samples specifically and record defects in tables. These tables then provided information to the processing operator so that the defects can be prevented from being included in assembly (Hallam et al., 2010).

Deming was interested in Shewhart's ideas and later they collaborated to develop an industrial quality improvement method. He further developed the Shewhart cycle. The Shewhart cycle was a cycle of steps for improving processes in an organization. Walter Shewhart first introduced this cycle in 1939. In 1950, Deming changed this cycle into four components of product design, product creation, product placement on the market, and re-design (DMPR). Deming then presented DMPR to JUSE in Japan (Wawak, 2018).

Deming introduced the Shewhart cycle in two versions (Keller and Pizdek, 2013). The first was a concise version with four elements, taught to the executive groups. This cycle consisted of designing, manufacturing, sales, research, and service. Meanwhile, for a group of engineers, Deming delivered an eight-stage cycle, consisting of the following:

1. Idea to emphasize on quality
2. Responsible to quality
3. Research
4. Design standard and product improvement to quality
5. Manufacture economically
6. Product inspection
7. Repair
8. Sales channel expansion

Deming then observed that Japanese made a separate Shewhart cycle which basically consisted of four steps, namely, plan, do, check, and act (PDCA). More precisely, it is the Japanese version of Shewhart cycle which includes four steps (Roser, 2016):

1. *Keikaku*: plan, project, schedule, scheme, program
2. *Jisshi*: enforcement, implementation, putting into practice, carrying out, operating, working
3. Check
4. Action

Deming then changed the term check to study, since, according to him, Japanese version of study is more suitable than checking (Gorenflo & Moran, 2010). In addition, the use of word "study" emphasizes that the steps were taken to create new knowledge (Wawak, 2018). Therefore, PDSA or PDCA cycle, known today, does not come from Deming or Shewhart, but from practices conducted in Japan.

Deming introduced management principles to be a foundation for the managers in creating a culture of continuous improvement. Deming's philosophy was "management work is working on a system to achieve continuous improvement of products and processes". Leaders must work as early as possible to develop an organization with a speedy pace to encourage quality improvement continuously. This includes breaking down cross-departmental boundaries (Zarbo, 2012).

The formula proposed by Deming comprised 14 management principles (Gabay, 2012):

1. Create constancy of purpose for improving products and services
2. Adopt the new philosophy
3. Cease dependence on mass inspection
4. End the practice of awarding business on price alone
5. Improve constantly and forever every system for production and service
6. Institute training on the job
7. Adopt and institute leadership
8. Drive out fear
9. Break down barriers in-between staff areas
10. Eliminate slogans, exhortations, and target for the workforce
11. Eliminate numerical quotas
12. Remove barriers that rob people of pride of workmanship
13. Encourage education and self-improvement program for everyone
14. Take action to accomplish transformation

Deming saw that Toyota was on the right track. Toyota had the right philosophical and managerial basis to encourage, support, and maintain quality by designing a system to do the right thing correctly since the first time they started producing (Zarbo, 2012).

According to Deming, if quality became a control force for culture, it would encourage efficiency, productivity, reduce costs, and in turn, allow companies to reduce price and attract more market share, increase profits, and customer satisfaction. For the production, quality would give award to human and its development, as well as enable a culture of respect, empowerment, and encourage employee accountability to develop. Employees would be appreciated for their expertise and knowledge (Zarbo, 2012).

Based on the contribution of Ford, Deming, Japanese tradition, and comparative studies conducted by Ohno in 1988, he published *Toyota Production System: Beyond Large Scale Production.* In his book, Ohno acknowledged the source of knowledge in compiling TPS. Ohno stated

> We have learned a lot from the United States automotive empire. America has produced amazing production management and business management techniques, such as quality control (QC), total quality control (TQC), and industrial engineering (IE). Japan imported these ideas and applied it. Japanese people shall not forget that these techniques were born in America and raised by the hard work of Americans. (Haak, 2004)

Ohno introduced two supporting pillars for TPS: JIT and autonomization. JIT, as previously explained, is a principle that states the right part in the assembly would only reach the line when it was required. This resulted in the product flow with almost zero inventory (Haak, 2006).

Autonomization or *jidoka* is an automation with human touch. Human touch here means human in an automatic stopping tool. The reason is, when there is an error in an automatic system, the system will immediately stop. The system would only run again if the problem is found and deleted. If there is no human monitoring, then this system would continue to stop until there are people who realize and fixe it (Haak, 2004). Human would look for the mistakes and correct them. However, the identification process and problem-solving take a long time and result in waste. Placement of a human as a stop device automatically would solve this problem. Human would immediately find the problem at the right point. As a result, there was almost no identification since the problem was revealed itself. Problem-solving could also be immediately implemented because the operator knows what to do.

This automatic stop tool was installed on almost all engines in Toyota, either new or old. In addition, these tools were also equipped with various safety equipment, fixed position stop, full working system, and *baka-yoke* system, which is an anti-error system for preventing defected products. Ohno emphasized that it basically gave "human intelligence, or human touch, to the machine" (Haak, 2006).

In 1990, two years after Ohno revealed the secret of Toyota, Womack, Jones, and Ross published *The Machine that Changed the World*. Womack, Jones, and Ross were three researchers from the Massachusetts Institute of Technology. They examined Japan's success in production management.

Using this book, Womack and his colleagues caught western attention to TPS. Womack and Jones's book has made scientists of production, industry managers, and management researchers aware of Japanese production management. This in turn led to further research. From psychological standpoint, Womack, Jones, and Ross's book provided a better view of how Japan succeeded in the industry. For Japan, Womack's book enhanced its image in the international community (Haak, 2004).

According to the three authors, TPS basically has five goals (Hallam, Muesel, & Flannery, 2010):

1. Precisely determine value with specific product
2. Identify value stream of each product
3. Create value stream without interruption
4. Let customers attract value from the manufacturer
5. Pursue perfection

In this book, "lean" was first used to describe TPS. Womack and Jones distinguished lean and TPS based on their specification only. Lean is TPS adjusted to be used on all companies in any industry. Both lean and TPS basically have the same elements. For example, lean principles according to Womack, Jones, and Ross are almost the same as TPS principles, which are (Haak, 2004)

1. Decide customer value
2. Decide value stream
3. Make the value flows
4. Make attractive from the customer's perspective
5. Strive for achieving perfection

Womack, Jones, and Ross then reported the results of their comparative study. This study compared Japanese, European, and US companies. They found that Toyota's strengths laid in three aspects: technology leadership, cost leadership, and time leadership. These three things were achieved by lean. Lean can produce these three advantages because it combines machine and human factors. The West failed to achieve excellence because they only relied on machine factors. Combination of human and machine completes each other while highlighting the strengths. The use of machinery allows mass production, but it creates flexibility issues. On the other hand, cost is quite a fortune to balance with the mass production system, but it has high flexibility. Workers with high skills become the human factors. They worked manually to manage machines that produce standardized products (Haak, 2006).

Based on their research on lean excellence, Womack et al. listed the characteristics of lean-based production according to the advantages of this hybrid system compared with Western mass production system. These advantages include the following (Haak, 2006):

1. Less defects in car manufacturing
2. Faster manufacture process
3. Smaller repair areas in company
4. Fewer supplies in company
5. Majority of employees work in groups
6. Workers often alternate jobs within the company in the production lines
7. Workers give more suggestion and are trained longer
8. Flat organizational structure

In 1998, Rother and Shook published the book *Learning to See*. This book attempts to expand lean application and conceptualization. According to Rother and Shook, the key activity in becoming lean is understanding and managing the flow of products, services, and activities which add value and do not add value to the product development (Aslanzadeh & Davoodi, 2014).

In line with this process, Rother and Shook introduced the concept of value stream mapping (VSM). In fact, the *Learning to See* is a book that has become the guidelines in the procedure of mapping the value stream in production. VSM is applied to display material and information in a process from the beginning to its end visually. This process is useful for modeling and improving the value stream. Visualization is performed to facilitate understanding, communication, and improvement process to improve efficiency. VSM uses icons, symbols, and standardized diagram-making principles (Figure 2.2). These elements are then used to display characteristics

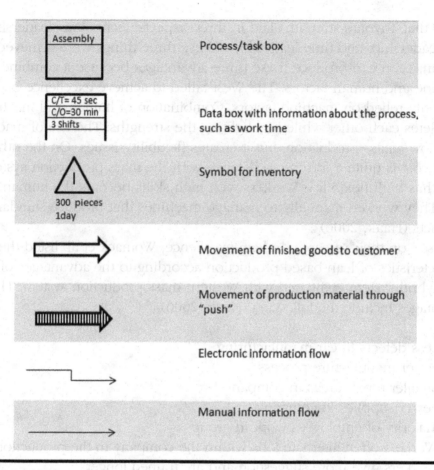

Figure 2.2 VSM symbols and notations (Aslanzadeh and Davoodi, 2014).

in a process that adds value or not. VSM allows these characteristics to be described as a whole in the process, rather than in individual isolated operation as the previous (Aslanzadeh and Davoodi, 2014).

After Rother and Sook introduced VSM, many adaptations were performed by latter authors. These adaptations were directed to more specific objectives in developing products (Aslanzadeh and Davoodi, 2014).

Chapter 3

Focus of Lean

Focus means target and the starting point to start another work. From the previous chapter on history of lean, we know that there is a focus shifting in lean development. In the Ford era, the focus was on automation and mass production. When Deming appeared, the focus shifted to quality. The development of directed organization was no longer about producing as many products as possible, but producing quality products even if they have to sacrifice quantity. After Ohno appeared, it shifted to autonomization and just-in-time. Just-in-time focuses on quantity because it produces the number of products according to customer attraction. Autonomization focuses on quality since it prevents defective components from being included in the value stream. After Ohno, Womack et al. introduced the lean concept. So, what is bigger than quantity and quality? Something that became the focus of lean? If lean is interpreted the same as Toyota Production System (TPS), the focus might be the same, which is quantity and quality of the product. However, lean is wider than TPS because it covers all organization and products. Of course, it does not only emphasize on quantity and quality.

First, focus may present in various dimensions. Quantity and quality are only a number and a dimension, respectively. We can take a look at another dimension such as location. Where lean is on location? Is it at the front office, back office, lower employee level, managerial level, leadership level, or overall level of the organization? Many organizations implementing lean still focus on the basic level (Hines et al., 2006). Even so, if lean is a method of improving business quality, it should focus on the widest possible level in an organization, which is the organization itself. This focus covers various aspects, not only the production but also supply chain, product development, administration, and behavior (Bhasin & Burcher, 2006). By using this comprehensive focus, the benefits of lean can be fully achieved (Bhasin & Burcher, 2006).

However, one should keep in mind that lean focuses on the autonomization approach. Meaning, it combines human and engine components. If we are talking only about the organization, then it is only related to the structure. Organization should be seen as a group of people working together. The widest interactional component of humans is culture. We know the term organizational culture as the highest level in organizational behavior. Therefore, by applying this logic, the focus of lean is only on organizational culture. We call the organizational culture that supports lean as *lean culture*.

Another issue needs to be considered is stakeholders. There are many stakeholders in the organization. Stakeholders include owners, shareholders, managers, employees, customers, business partners (suppliers, distributors), and community in general. Who does lean give its focus? If we stand on practical level, lean leads to the effort of eliminating waste systematically from the organization operation through a set of synergic working practices to manufacture products and services on demand (Yang, Hong, & Modi, 2011). The components that reflect stakeholders are managers and customers. Managers are stakeholders who conduct waste elimination process. Nevertheless, the main focus is not on the manager. Note the last part of this statement: on demand. Whose demand? Absolutely, the customer demand. However, since the waste elimination is the effort to manufacture products and services for customers on demand, the main focus lies on the customers. Meaning that, the focus on stakeholder level is focusing on customers.

Why the customers need products and services? Because they are valuable to customers. Products and services are needed to meet the customer needs and demands. Products will be more preferred if it provides value to them. Therefore, the more specific focus of lean lies on this value. In other words, the focus of lean is *customer value*.

Again, the practical focus of lean is waste reduction (Timans, Antony, Ahaus, & Van Solingen, 2012). Reduction is a verb. It is not an input or output, but a process of converting input into output. Focus on input is rarely conducted by organizations. Business organizations generally focus on their output or products. However, lean focusses on the process. In a system, lean works by focusing on ongoing process in the form of waste reduction. Nahmens and Ikuma (2012) state that one of the key focuses of lean is eliminating waste from the processes. Therefore, the focus is in the *process*.

Based on the discussion above and in the previous chapter, we identified five focuses of lean:

1. At the spectrum between human and machines, lean focuses on humans and machines at once. This is different from Ford's idea, which focusses on machines, and Deming's idea, focusing on humans.
2. At the spectrum between quantity and quality, lean focuses on quantity and quality at once. It is different from Ford, who focuses on quantity, and Deming, who focuses on quality.
3. At the spectrum between human organization levels, lean focuses on the broadest level, that is on organizational culture. Since the focus lies on culture, automatically, at temporal spectrum, lean also focuses on long-term issues rather than the shorter ones. In fact, short-term achievements can be sacrificed for long-term achievements.
4. At the spectrum of various types of stakeholders, lean focuses on customers. Lean focuses on the efforts to increase customer value.
5. At the spectrum of system, that is input–output process, lean focuses on the process. Lean tries to eliminate waste due to the process.

Figure 3.1 indicates the focus of lean in an organization.

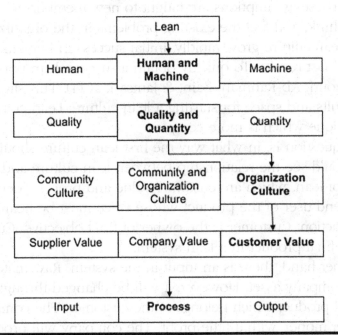

Figure 3.1   Focus of lean.

The first two focuses in the explanation above have been discussed in the previous chapter. We will here explain the other three focuses of lean: lean culture, customer value, and focus of process.

Lean Culture

The widely accepted definition of organizational culture is the definition given by Schein. Schein states that culture is

> A pattern of shared basic assumptions that the group learned as it solved problems, that has worked well enough to be considered valid and, therefore, to be taught to new members as the correct way to perceive, think, and feel in relation to those problems. (Höök, 2008)

Lean culture is the culture behind lean implementation. From Schein's definition, this culture has shared assumptions that are proven successful, and known as the best way to think and act based on lean concepts. In this definition, organization members develop a lean culture after several times of successful lean implementation. Success then forms a common basic assumption. These assumptions are taught to new members as the best way to perceive, think, and feel the existing problems in the organization.

To make lean culture grow rapidly, initial success in implementing lean must produce fast results. To quickly obtain a success, lean practice must be simple (Manzouri, Ab-Rahman, Zain, & Jamsari, 2014). This simplicity provides fast results and space for starting a lean culture. Lean culture will grow as lean technique which is more complex.

The next question is, in what way the first lean culture should be developed? We should see the relationship between lean culture and the other two focuses of lean, which are customer value and process focus. The customer is the end user of the product whose voice must be heard for a guidance to lean action. Customer is the owner of final objective. Customer is the owner of final product in a lean system.

On the other hand, there is an input in the system. Raw material as the input is the company asset. However, it will be changed through the process into final product which belongs to the customer. The company buys it with customer money with a little profit. The company will process it into a product to obtain more profit. This product is sold to the customer and this product is the result of the process.

The process point between input and output is under the authority of organization members. The organization members determine what would be the converting process of input into output. Therefore, since this process is determined entirely by the organization, organization members are the process owners. We say that the process in organization belongs to the organization members. Therefore, a good lean culture is a culture realizing that processes belong to them, and that they have the power to run lean in production process.

This seems easy, but many company members do not be aware of the process ownership. They work as they want and in less optimal way because they think the process does not belong to them. They do not want to think the best way to do something. They do not want to cooperate to improve the quality and quantity of production process.

The focus of lean culture is the *process ownership culture*. Toyota took 60 years to perfect their lean and most of the time was directed in establishing a culture of process ownership (Keif, 2006). Besides, since lean must be conducted sustainably, even Toyota is still working on establishing a culture of process ownership to date. They initiated it by studying the social system in lean process. Once this social system is understood, they develop a culture of process ownership. This development produces various issues such as organization member awareness to strive to be better, member awareness of personal responsibility for the process. While for management, they are committed to perform the right actions even though they are expensive and costly. Furthermore, a culture of process ownership will lead to the focus of a new lean culture, which is the culture of stopping production and correcting problems. This *baujinka* culture will guarantee the right quality from the beginning, so, the next task is fulfilling the quantity. This culture is different from common culture which will only stop when it is required, so that the work is not in vain (Kelf, 2006).

Process ownership culture is a required culture, so that continuous improvement can be performed (Moodaliyar, 2010). Each organization member is the process owner in certain parts of process. It means that each member has individual responsibilities in their respective fields. They are aware of their position in the process and they must use their authority and responsibility. Some people will have the same part of responsibility and each part is connected to each other by different people who are responsible for it. As a result, the ownership can function properly if anyone in a division or between divisions must work together. They work together to understand the whole process from upstream to downstream.

How does the process ownership occur? There are several strategies to take. Employees must be allowed to participate in decision-making process to improve organization performance. Since they are involved in the decision-making process, they would feel that they have a certain portion in running the process and have a sense of ownership. Managers have their own programs to engage employees to take a part in process of improvement strategy. They must be proactive. If they are passive, for example, by only providing an opinion box, the employees are probably less intrigued. Managers must see the employees directly to seek opinions from them. The managers must ask about their problems or take opinions about how the process can be made better. Employees must be invited to be involved in the problem-solving process using lean techniques. They should also be empowered to implement the solutions to the problems that are blocking the process. Their names should be recorded and given appreciation for their innovative ideas, both face-to-face or one by one or in a meeting. Managers must bend their ears not to oversee the employees but to listen their ideas (Childs, 2017).

If employees already have sense of ownership to the business process, they can easily accept changes. They will support and contribute to these changes. They will also be strongly committed to encourage the process of achieving sustainable organization improvement (Childs, 2017). It comes from the feeling that each of them has a portion in the production process. In other words, they are optimally empowered. They have become the real smallest part of an organization, working individually and in groups to achieve organization goals (Childs, 2017). This is not only for the benefit of shareholder/owner or customer benefits. A research indicates that process ownership has a positive effect on job satisfaction. The reason is the employees have authority over the work process so they feel that they have personal investment in the organization and hence feel satisfied (Childs, 2017).

Based on the earlier description, there are two main characteristics of process ownership culture. First, this is a culture of mutual respect. Managers appreciate subordinates, subordinates appreciate managers and fellow coworkers. Those appreciated are ideas, determination, opinions, and others through which they contribute to the process. Thus, *process ownership culture is a culture of mutual respect.*

Second, this culture is interactive. The interaction occurs among the group members and among the employees. Rewards without interaction will create a gap. Rewards accompanied with interaction will result in mutual support and mutual assistance in yielding a quality process. That is why lean emphasizes team collaboration to solve a problem while recognizing personal and group contribution. So, *ownership culture is an interactive culture.*

Customer Value

If the employees already feel that they contribute to a process, they are ready to achieve customer values. The concept of customer value is defined as "customer's overall assessment on the utility of a product based on the perceptions of what is received and what is given" (Oh, 1999).

There is a difference between what customer expected and what is valuable to them. Customers can expect some values but that demand is only a small part of their perceived value. Customer value is broader than customer demand. However, many organizations only see on their customer demand while do not try to understand what customers' value is.

An important indicator of whether something is valuable or not is when customers are willing to pay. If something is deemed invaluable by the customer, they are unwilling to pay for it, and even if they are forced to pay, they are not happy to pay for it. For example, queuing. Queuing to get services is definitely not valuable for the customers. Customers obviously do not want to queue to pay, if they have to queue, they are not happy. Queuing is not valuable for customers.

Lean works around customer value. The process is broken down and each part is considered as it is valuable or not. If it is not valuable, lean requires the process to be seen as a waste. In addition, some organization members, especially those who are responsible for the process, feel unhappy if it is said as a waste. However, labeling a process that is wasteful increases the whole organization members' awareness that the process must be handled immediately to make the value stream run smoothly.

For employees who think they have a wasteful process, they will be encouraged to be active in providing ideas and implementing improvement. Their involvement may be paradoxical, in the sense of removing their responsibilities. It might happen because the process will disappear from the value stream. Therefore, they must be appreciated. The reward should be to place them in a certain position within the organization. Probably they can be promoted or otherwise moved to a new process that really adds a new value.

Somehow not all processes that do not add value must be eliminated. These processes may be essential for the overall process. In this case, the employees are committed to keep the process always at a minimum level. For example, consider the previous example of queuing. An employee might be paid for managing the queue. Nevertheless, because it is a non-adding value process, the organization will always try to keep the queue short. This is the responsibility of the queue officers. They will be given a reward or bonus if the queue is always short. If they manage to keep no queue, they will obtain a bigger reward or bonus. The presence remains essential, even though the job is under the non-adding value process.

There is a fundamental difference between customer value–oriented process and other issue– oriented process. Other issue here is generally the internal production efficiency. The process that is focusing on internal production efficiency seeks to make the production process run as efficient as possible based on one correct value. There is only one value as the focus and the process serves that value as effective and efficient as possible. The processes are categorized into two groups, namely, providing-value process and non-providing value process. Non-providing value process will be cut to make the production efficient.

On the other hand, a production process oriented on customer value will be more dynamic. The process is divided into three groups, namely, adding-value process, providing-value process, and non-providing value process. Note that there is a new category, adding-value process. The value of a product can be added. This addition can occur if the company understands the unrevealed customer value. This makes lean different from the common production process. Lean will encourage people who stand at the point of business interface to observe what customers consider as valuable. If it identifies a new value, it will observe which process in the system is able to add new value and non-providing process value. Otherwise, whether the previous process which did not provide value to the old value will be able to add value.

In lean implementation, the concept of "adding value" requires customer surveys or observations on customer behavior in consuming products. These new values will be more or less integrated to the existing products. Otherwise, it becomes too far to be achieved. Customer values which are too far come under a separate department of research and development (R&D). R&D department will research and study how the existing process can add this very new value. This issue is under R&D because the newest values sometimes require large investment and addition of a new process apart from the existing process.

Besides seeing the fact whether customers are happy in paying for something, customer value can also be seen by making comparison between what they think is appropriate to obtain at a certain price and what they actually obtained. For example, when customers rent a room in a hotel for 1 million IDR (Indonesian Rupiah), they have an idea of what services the hotel will provide with 1 million IDR room. When they obtain the service, they can give an assessment of 1 to 6, where 1 means worse than their expectation, while 6 is much better than their expectation. High customer values occurred if they generally answer that they obtained much better services than their expectation (Oh, 1999). Another example is the process of queuing to buy in fast food restaurants. Customers might be happy to queue if the food is affordable and tasty. In this case, queuing is not considered as a waste because it compensates for the affordable food. However, if the restaurant wants to add the value to customer, indeed, the process of queuing can be considered as a waste. By using a better customer value, the restaurant can increase its selling price to the point which the customer views as worth.

Why does lean have to pursue customer values? Why lean is not satisfied enough with the efficiency of production process? It happens because customer value is related to numerous positive issues that can be obtained by the organization. Customer value is known to determine customer purchasing decision. The higher the customer value, the more the customers purchase. They will keep coming back to buy because they obtain satisfaction and high value. Moreover, high value will lead to customer satisfaction (Oh, 1999). If customers continue to make purchases, the organization already has a loyal customer base and does not need to worry about losing buyers as long as they are able to maintain customer value.

Moreover, customer value does not only give loyalty to existing customers but also encourage them to inform other people (Oh, 1999). The spreading story will encourage other people to become customers. As a result, the customer base will continue to grow over time. This in turn, increases business profits. Therefore, the business has achieved a sustainable benefit.

On the other hand, it is known that customer value is affected by three issues: price perception, quality perception, and performance perception (Oh, 1999). Price perception is the perception of price given to customers. Quality perception is the perception of goods/service quality provided. Performance perception is the perception of utility of goods/services to meet the customer needs. If the business can provide a low price, good service, and have a good-performance product, then the customer value will grow higher.

How does lean achieve these three goals? To provide a low price, the company must perform cost efficiency, and this process can be achieved through lean. To provide quality products/services, the company must also keep away from making mistakes in the production process. It is also achieved through lean. Furthermore, if the company wishes to provide high-performance products/services, the company must also review the most valuable aspect of the product from the customers' perspective. This process is also achieved using lean.

If the competitors provide the same quality of goods and services with more expensive price, the customers will absolutely choose goods with affordable price. If the competitors provide goods and services in the same price but in poorer quality, then customers will choose the company offering better-quality goods. In brief, focusing on customer value enables organization implementing lean to achieve sustainable excellence in the competition.

Focus on the Process

Focusing on process is inevitable in lean steps. Focusing on process allows the workforce to identify and eliminate waste from the system to satisfy the customers. In manufacturing, the process focus is on business process and process management. Meanwhile, in the service companies, the process focus is inseparable part from the marketing and operational resources (Hult, 2011). In both commodities, goods and services, the process focus is very important to be implemented.

A process can be categorized based on the complexity and intensity (Setia, Venkatesh, & Joglekar, 2013). A complex process requires great attention because a lot of waste is hidden beneath. A complex process is characterized by non-routine processes, high level of difficulty, full of uncertainty, and interdependencies among the divisions. This type of process requires a quality supply to facilitate the running process. Variations in supply quality will result in waste in a complex process. More attention needs to be given to identify the occurring waste in this complex process.

Meanwhile, process intensity is the amount of resources needed to effectively manage business process activities (Setia et al., 2013). Process with high intensity will tend to have waste on the supply. High-intensity process may also produce a lot of waste in many large resource managements. The point is the more complex and intensive a process is, the greater the existence of waste; thus it is important to run lean to eliminate that waste.

The consequence of focus on lean process initiative is the various restructuring efforts to streamline the process including the factory layout as it can be seen from various efforts such as reorganizing the installation, cellular layout, etc. (Demeter & Matyusz, 2011).

Indeed, focusing on the process is not the only lean domination. However, there are only two options: focus on the product or focus on the process. There are some organizations that focus on the process, even if they do not adopt lean. Therefore, Demeter and Matyusz (2011) indicate that lean companies are more focused on process than the companies that do not adopt lean.

The process focus on lean is not only indicated in restructuring process but also in various steps. The point is lean requires attention on each step of the process. At each step, lean labels whether the step adds value or not. Lean views that a more effective way to improve quality is by identifying waste in the process. This seems simple but actually it was not considered many times in the previous thoughts. Fillingham (2007) observes that 99% of traditional management approaches are more focused on providing small increases in measures that add value while ignoring measures that do not add value. Lean works the other way around, it looks at the non-adding value steps and then eliminates them. This is what distinguishes the process focus on lean with other management approaches.

Fillingham (2007) justifies the ability of lean to improve process effectively than other traditional management approaches. The reason is that there are too many non-adding value steps in the process. Fillingham (2007) estimates that the ratio of non-adding value steps to adding value steps is 9:1. Meaning that, out of 10 processes, there are 9 non-adding value processes and only 1 adding value step.

The focus on adding value has the consequences of the narrow view of the whole process. If someone sees that the process steps under his/her responsibility have added value, then he/she will focus to increase that value. Conversely, if the focus is to identify non-adding value steps, the management must look at all the steps in the process and identify which steps are the non-adding value steps.

Fillingham (2009) provides an example of hospital. At the hospital, each department tends to focus on the process of increasing the adding value steps. As a result, the overall process is often unknown to the healthcare personnel in the hospital. Often, only patients themselves can feel the whole process. Moreover, the most problematic process lies in the departments of administration and information, which are five or six times more complex than other processes.

The result of focusing on adding value steps is the emergence of various mistakes, duplications, and delays (Fillingham, 2009). Each tries to add temporary value clandestinely, but then non-adding value steps are dominating. As a result, frontline staff feel that their efforts are in vain. They have worked hard to improve their service quality, but the patients still cannot feel the overall high quality. This occurs solely because of failure to focus on more important steps in manufacturing products or services.

In summary, we have learned that focus of lean lies in three practical issues, namely, lean culture, customer value, and process. Lean demands the old organizational culture to be ceased and transformed into a lean culture, focusing on the process ownership with more respectful and interactive way. Lean also requires that organization members focus on the customer demands to produce valuable processes and products for them. Lean in turn focuses on eliminating waste to produce high-value products for customers, rather than increasing efficient steps (not wasteful) from the beginning. Next, we will discuss what lean process looks like.

Chapter 4

What is Lean Process?

Lean process is a process that uses only the absolute minimum resources to add value on services or products (Kang & Apte, 2007). George (2003) provides an exact definition. According to him, lean process is a process with a value-added time of more than 20% of the total cycle time in a production process. The value of 20% is a moderate value, as the average business process only has 5% of total cycle time to add value. The remaining 95% is only waiting time in the process. If the company can reach 25% efficiency, it can be said as international class. Table 4.1 lists the average cycle efficiency of various processes.

Lean process lowers the cost of products or services because it uses minimum resources. The resource minimization is achieved through two basic principles of lean process: waste identification and waste elimination (Nakayama & Mgbike, 2010). Therefore, the main questions to start lean process are (1) where is the biggest waste of resources in the ongoing process? These resources can be time, human, and material. (2) How can we minimize this waste? (Nakayama and Mgbike, 2010).

Table 4.1   Non-Lean Process Cycle Efficiency

Application	Typical Cycle Efficiency	World Class Cycle Efficiency
Sustainable manufacture	5%	30%
Business process (service)	10%	50%
Business process (creative/cognitive)	5%	25%

Source: George (2003).

The development of lean process certainly requires investment and this investment can be quite large (Morgan & Company, 2011). For some parties, this investment might be seen as a form of waste. However, the investment on the lean process will provide benefits because its main target is reducing waste. Profits are obtained if the investment value is much smaller than the amount of reduced waste. Waste elimination allows the addition of customer value that, as previously explained, leads to customer loyalty and new customer acquisition.

An example of a successful lean implementation is not only in Toyota. Liker and Morgan (2011), for instance, reported how Dearborn Tool and Die, a tool shop, made a big profit because of investment in lean process, supported by digital technology. The profits were gained from the transition of metal and production models that changed from traditional handy model to high-precision and machine-intensive lean model.

Ford case also indicates the ability of lean to achieve success in the market (Liker and Morgan, 2011). Ford had previously invested in increasing the work team members' accountability, in accordance with the company's general strategy (see Figure 4.1). Without a lean process, this high accountability of work team cannot provide maximum result, and might become wasteful. By using lean, this work team is able to work using their best focused and standardized working spirit because their skills are used in an ideal work setting without waste.

Liker and Morgan (2011) concluded that lean process increases effectiveness in encouraging high-quality, low-cost, and short-waiting-time products. Waste identification is the first step in the process to indicate problems to the surface so that it immediately leads to problem-solving. Moreover, because lean process is sustainable, then over time, waste identification is faster and the solutions are more quickly exposed and applied. Therefore, overall, it indicates an increasing speed in problem-solving. In other words, the turnaround in plan, do, check, act (PDCA) cycle goes faster.

An important tool in identifying this waste is value stream mapping (VSM). At the initial stage, there is no VSM so it takes a long time to create the VSM. After the VSM is available, in the next PDCA cycle, we only need to refer to VSM to make the process run faster. Furthermore, organization

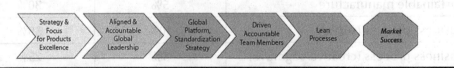

Figure 4.1   Ford's market successful keys (Liker and Morgan, 2011).

members become used to in understanding how to fix problems, thus solving problems becomes even faster. Meanwhile, fewer problems will be found because they have been resolved in the previous process. The potential problems that disappear can be large since lean is directed at the root problems to raise many branch problems (Crawford, 2006). The solution to the root problems certainly eliminates branch problems.

Important basic concepts in lean process are as follows (Wojtys, Schley, Overgaard, & Agbabian, 2009):

1. Value: The executive identifies what the customer considers valuable. This value is specific to the product or service and can only be determined by the customers.
2. Stream: Organization executives and members develop a value stream reflecting each step in the production of products or services. Waste is identified and eliminated from this value stream. The final result is an efficient product flow. To guarantee this stream, supervision and management of the process is conducted and supported by visual controls. These tools can indicate the status of various items or services in the process (George, 2003).
3. Attraction: Customers attract the product values almost without hindrance or delay. According to George (2003), lean system uses pull system where new jobs are released into the process only when the job has been stimulated from the customer side to move forward to the next process. To guarantee this process, a maximum limit for the amount of work in process is made, so the process speed can be controlled (George, 2003).
4. Perfection: If obstacle or delay still exists, it means there is waste. The step of improving value stream should be implemented. In fact, obstacle or delay will always exist, but in smaller number. As a result, lean process will run continuously to perfection.

Figures 4.2 and 4.3 indicate the examples of value stream map before and after lean process. Note that the flow chart after the lean process was made even before the lean process was conducted. This map is called future state VSM. The function of future state VSM is visualizing the future VSM after lean process runs, so that targets can be more easily achieved.

The comparison between the initial VSM and the future state VSM indicates the amount of waste in the initial VSM. There are nine steps in initial VSM, while the final VSM consists of only five steps. The required

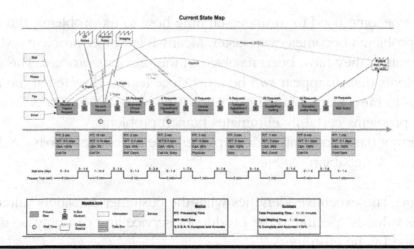

Figure 4.2 VSM example (Wojtys et al., 2009).

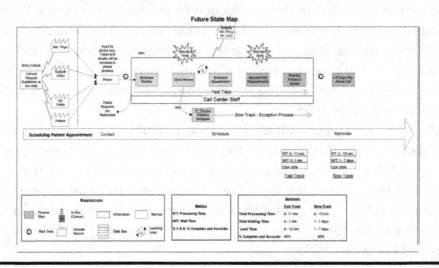

Figure 4.3 Future state VSM example (Wojtys et al., 2009).

investment to introduce lean process to staffs, arrange schedule, develop VSM, and take corrective actions in the case above is for 10 days.

This result of investment is very satisfying. In the initial situation, a patient needs at least 5 minutes for calling the clinic and the process can take up to 21 minutes, for 36 days. After the lean process, the first call only takes 2.5 minutes on average and 75% of patients even make one phone call before treated by a doctor (Wojtys et al., 2009).

Another example of success was presented by Monteiro, Pacheco, Dinis-Carvalho, and Paiva (2015) in the public affairs office case. The various processes produced were faster without reducing its quality. Table 4.2 indicates how progress is achieved with lean process in public affairs case.

Table 4.2   Process Improvement in Waste Management Office

Process	Before Lean (June 2010)	After Lean (December 2010)	Recent (2015)
Management reporting (days)	3	2	2
Monthly account closing (days)	8	6	4.5
Wage processing (days)	10	5	5
Payment to suppliers (days)	9	3.5	1.5
Direct handling (days)	5	3	0.5

Source: Monteiro et al. (2015).

Another example can be found in Murman (2003). Murman reports a drastic change in the process of airlines. Before lean, the process reached 27 stages. Lean cut the stages to make it only to five stages.

The illustration above clearly shows that lean process provides great benefits of faster, more efficient, more economical, and higher-quality processes (Afrin & Islam, 2018). These benefits are inherently embedded in the purpose of lean process. The aim of lean process is to manufacture products and services at the lowest cost and with the highest possible speed (Antony, 2011).

Chapter 5

Why Should Organizations Use Lean?

There are at least two important reasons for organizations to use lean: substantially cutting costs and providing competitive advantage (Andersson, Eriksson, & Torstensson, 2006). Basically, an organization chooses lean because of its benefits. Therefore, it can be said that lean can cut costs and provide a competitive advantage for the organization.

In 2003, NIST (National Institute of Standards and Technology) in the United States conducted a survey on 40 manufacturing companies that used lean. They found that there were three fields indicating remarkable increases due to lean implementation (Andersson et al., 2006):

1. Operational: The improvements found were lead time reduction, productivity increase, reduction of work inventory in the process, inventory transition increase, capacity increase, cycle time reduction, etc.
2. Administrative: The improvements include order processing error reduction, streamlining customer service function so the customers do not need to wait longer, etc.
3. Strategic: Improvements in strategic areas include costs reduction, etc.

Alves, Dinis-Carvalho, Sousa, Moreira, and Lima (2011) conducted a survey on 14 companies in Portugal that applied lean. They found that there were various kinds of benefits gained due to lean implementation. Table 5.1 is quite long but is important to indicate the benefits of lean.

Table 5.1 Lean Benefits in the Portuguese Companies

Company	Project	Device	Benefits	Year
A	Organization and optimization of cutting sector using just-in-time (JIT) device	JIT	Replacement time reduction (27%) Material flow simplification First in, first out implementation Reduction of required space One shift elimination	2001
	Organization and optimization of cutting sector using single minute exchange of dies (SMED) and 5S (sort, straighten, shine, standardize, sustain)	SMED, 5S	Replacement time reduction (40%) Wasting time reduction Lot size reduction (from 200 to 50 components) Engine performance improvement	2001
B	Kanban System Implementation	Kanban	The process becomes more transparent and easier to be controlled Kanban box implementation Reduction of work in process (from 6 to 2 hours)	2005
	Performance comparison between assembly lines and assembly cells	Overall equipment effectiveness (OEE)	OEE measurement implementation	2005
	Work rotation implementation	Indicators of Labour productivity	Productivity improvement (20%)	2005
	Quick replacement implementation	Quick replacement	Replacement time reduction (around 50% in the main equipment of assembly line) Reduction of work in process (36%) Time reduction from standard work adoption	2006

(Continued)

Table 5.1 (Continued) Lean Benefits in the Portuguese Companies

Company	Project	Device	Benefits	Year
	Point continuous improvement process (CIP)	Point CIP	General improvement	2006
	Standard work implementation	Standard work	Productivity improvement (30%)	2007
	Point CIP implementation	Point CIP	General improvement	2007
	Productivity improvements in heat control assembly cells	Cell	Movement time reduction Cell governance improvement	2008
	Implementation of production lifting in a tensile environment	Production lifting	Final product supply reduction (20%) Bonded capital saving (around 18,000 Euro) Approaching every part, every interval (EPEI); ideal EPEI=1 Approaching to weekly daily lifting meeting at a very close value to the ideal value (100%) Achievement of negotiation deadlines with clients in 97% of cases	2008
	Alternative layout analysis in car radio assembly line	Layout analysis, sustainable improvement	Reduction of work in process (211 to 107 car radios) Employees reduction (27 to 21 workers) Reduction of covered area (358 to 252 m^2)	2008
	Performance improvement of work team in the final cell of car radio assembly	Team work	Cells organization improvement change the operation mode Moving time reduction	2009

(Continued)

Table 5.1 (*Continued*) Lean Benefits in the Portuguese Companies

Company	Project	Device	Benefits	Year
	Ship-to-line implementation	Ship-to-line	Eliminate warehouse area Transport time reduction Movement time reduction Reduction of one transporting vehicle	2010
	Kanban system development in electronic components cell assembly	Pull system, *Kanban*, cell	Space reduction (80 to 66 m²) Changes to standard work Cycle time reduction from one work station (47 seconds to 35 seconds) Moving time reduction Cells organization improvement	2010
	Capacity planning and scheduling operations in the material supply warehouses	Capacity planning	Creating a model for calculating the required HR in the warehouse for supply assembly lines	2010
C	Lean manufacture application in logistics – raw materials supply	Lean logistic, standard work	Unloading of trucks time reduction Product identification time reduction in warehouse Wasted time reduction in movement Human work reduction Standard procedure for warehouse work	2009
	Lean manufacture application in logistics – expedition	Lean logistic	Activity decreasing without value Productivity improvement (26%) Packaging standards to reduce client complaints Increasing warehouse flow for final goods	2009
	Setup time reduction	SMED	Setup reduction (60%)	2009

(Continued)

Table 5.1 (Continued)   Lean Benefits in the Portuguese Companies

Company	Project	Device	Benefits	Year
D	Principle implementation and lean manufacture practice in metal mechanic companies	5S, *Poka Yoke*, pull system, cells, *kaizen*, value stream mapping (VSM)	Distance reduction (25%) through cell layout reconfiguration Waiting time reduction (80%) Moving time reduction	2010
E	Production cell implementation	5S, *Kanban*, TBS (Temporary Build Sequence), SMED, cell	General improvement	2008
	Pull system implementation in the electronic components assembly lines	Pull system, VSM	Waiting time reduction (31%) Work in process reduction (18%, €7,600) Queue time reduction (82%) Defective work in process reduction (35%) Reworking cost reduction (€2,591)	2010
	Cell assembly implementation and lean manufacture practices in the electronic component companies	Cell, VSM	Reconfiguration of 5 assembly lines into 2 cells by space (50%) and workers reduction (minus 2) Work center occupational repair Work in process reduction (8.2 to 1.3 days) Waiting time reduction	2010

(Continued)

Table 5.1 (Continued) Lean Benefits in the Portuguese Companies

Company	Project	Device	Benefits	Year
	Lean manufacture technique implementation in supply management for production lines and sub-contracts	Pull system, *Kanban*	Distance reduction (20%) Total movement reduction (24%) Work in process reduction (36%, €8,137) Waiting time reduction (80%)	2010
	SMED implementation in the production of plastic and metal components	SMED	Setup time reduction in three working stations (188.15 to 77.8 minutes; 61.8 to 6.35 minutes; 58.14 to 9.8 minutes) Work in process reduction (17.05 to 7.74 days, €318.75 to €144.38) Movement reduction (370 to 10 m, 260 to 2 m)	2010
F	Lean game development as a tool to introduce lean attitudes on the shop floor	Lean game	Improvement in training effectiveness	2008
G	Lean manufacture application to improve lab performance	5S, pull stream	Evaluated performance, bottleneck is identified, and work in process reduction	2008
H	Kanban system development and implementation in metallurgical companies	*Kanban*	Independent material flow Production lifting Visual management Temporary supply reduction	2010
I	Production cell supply	*Kanban pull system*	More transparent process Easier to be controlled *Kanban* system implementation Material reserve reduction Supply failure reduction	2006

(Continued)

Table 5.1 (*Continued*)   Lean Benefits in the Portuguese Companies

Company	Project	Device	Benefits	Year
J	Bosch production system dissemination and *Kanban* implementation	*Kanban*, visual management	Work in process reduction Planning task release in the production division	2005
	Reconfiguration of product-oriented manufacturing systems	Cell	More transparent process Increased flexibility Simpler material flow and supply Waste identification and elimination is easier	2007
	Performance improvements in packaging division	Point CIP	Cycle time reduction (6%)	2010
K	Climate control panel assembly line increasing (automotive industry)	Line balance, visual management	Efficiency improved (75.13% to 90.87%) Cost reduction (€33,600/year)	2004
L	Analysis, simplification, and implementation of processes in bus agency companies	Sustainable improvement	Quality improvement (noise level in the bus) Repainting work reduction Cost reduction (€6,156/bus)	2008
M	Analysis and improvement of fluorescent advertising sign production system	Standard work, 5S, layout analysis	Standard worksheet implementation Financing system Implementation Productivity improvement Quality improvement (fewer customer complaints)	2005
N	Cell production implementation	Cell	General improvement	2007

Source: Alves et al. (2011).

Chapter 6

Consequences of Poor Quality

Any manufactured product or service by the production process has a certain zone in quality. If the company works without improving quality, its quality tends to become poor, and sometimes the company has to increase costs of the poor-quality products. This sporadic increase occurs when there are defective products entering the market. The more the sporadic increases in cost of poor quality, the lower the average product quality. Juran (1986) presents this situation in graphical form (Figure 6.1).

Note that at the beginning of operation, cost level of poor quality is at level 20 and fluctuates over time. Over time, the fluctuation increases negatively. It means that the cost of poor quality becomes greater when there is a fluctuation. In the example above, fluctuation leads to the cost of poor

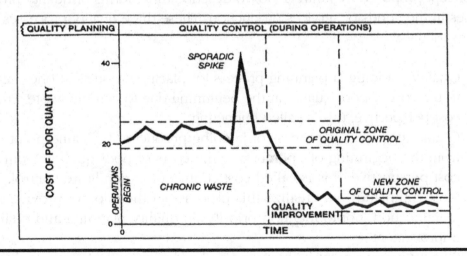

Figure 6.1   Quality trilogy (Juran, 1986).

quality reaching 40 points. Due to this fluctuation, the product is in a zone of quality control higher than 20.

This fluctuation rarely reduces cost of poor quality. This is due to chronic waste. Chronic waste tends to accumulate over time. Chronic waste cannot be removed without awareness to suppress it. Due to upward trend in chronic waste, the cost of quality costs is getting worse, shifting the quality control zone. Without quality improvement, over time, the quality costs will reach a high average. It is not impossible if at a time the quality control zone reaches an average cost of 40.

Based on this trend, quality improvement is required. Conceptual quality improvement will reduce cost of poor quality. Intervention such as lean is a form of quality improvement. Quality improvement will reduce the average cost of poor quality, let us say to level 5 from level 20. In addition, quality improvement will reduce variation, and therefore provides smaller fluctuation possibility.

Obviously, if the quality improvement is only implemented once, the costs of poor quality rise will re-occur. In the long run, the costs of poor quality may return to level 20 even though it is not as fast as before. Therefore, to prevent the rising trends, there must be a continuous quality improvement. An effective continuous quality improvement will not only suppress cost of poor quality to rise but also suppress the quality control zone to further decrease, as shown in Figure 6.1. It means, it will further reduce the cost of poor quality.

Figure 6.1 introduces the concept of quality trilogy. The quality trilogy is a concept proposed by Juran (1986) to describe three forms of quality processes in the goods or services production. These three quality processes are as follows:

1. Quality planning, a planning process for placing products at one point in the cost of poor quality at the beginning due to chronic waste. From cost perspective, this is called budgeting.
2. Quality control, the process of keeping product at the same point from the beginning of operation at the costs of poor quality. From cost perspective, this is called cost control or expenditure control. Most companies only realize this process but they do not provide identification, not to mention priority on quality planning and quality improvement.
3. Quality improvement is the process of reducing cost of poor quality by eliminating chronic waste and preventing sporadic spikes in poor

quality. From cost perspective, this is referred as cost reduction or profit improvement.

Juran (1986) observed that the Western products' quality has decreased due to lack of attention to improve their quality. On the other hand, the Japanese products' quality is significantly increasing as they emphasize on improving the quality. In the mid-1970s, Japanese products' quality had outperformed the Western products' quality. This is amazing considering that in 1950, Japanese products' quality was far below the Western products. During his visit to Japan, Juran (1986) observed that steel companies in Japan only had costs of poor quality of 1–2% of sales, while in the United States, steel companies had to face cost of poor quality of 10–15%. United States entrepreneurs did not even believe in the small value of poor-quality cost. This is indicated in Figure 6.2.

Cost of poor quality is a part of quality cost concept. The concept of quality cost was first introduced by Armand Feigenbaum in 1943 (Schiffauerova & Thomson, 2006). There are two types of quality costs, namely, cost of good quality and cost of poor quality. Cost of good quality, also called discretionary cost, compliance cost, or quality control cost, is an investment cost to make the product quality always in the good condition. This cost includes prevention cost and appraisal cost (Gupta & Campbell, 1995).

Prevention cost is incurred cost to avoid quality problems. This cost includes the following (Oakland, 2003):

1. Product or service requirement costs
2. Quality planning cost
3. Quality report cost

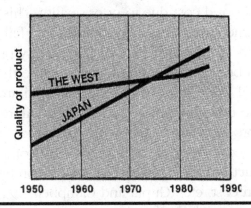

Figure 6.2 Western versus Japanese quality competition during 1950–1985 (Juran, 1986).

4. Quality warranty cost
5. Supplier quality warranty cost
6. Inspection equipment cost: design, development, and/or equipment purchase for inspection
7. Quality improvement cost
8. Quality control system cost
9. New product development reviewing cost
10. Training cost
11. Other costs: domestic work, supply, shipping, communication, and general affairs activities related to quality

Assessment cost is the cost incurred by the company to ensure that the product reaches a specified quality standard. Assessment cost includes the following (Oakland, 2003):

1. Raw material inspection cost
2. Verification cost
3. Quality audit cost
4. Inspection equipment cost for calibration and equipment maintenance used in all inspection activities
5. Testing cost
6. Calibration cost
7. Work in process assessment cost
8. Rating vendor cost
9. Final goods inspection cost

Poor quality cost, also called consequential cost, non-compliance cost, or failure cost, is the incurred cost due to poor quality. This cost includes internal failure cost and external failure cost. Internal failure cost is received when a company fails to manufacture a certain quality product. This cost is said to be internal because the failure occurs before the product reaches the customer. Internal failure cost includes product failure cost, downgrading cost, rework cost, downtime cost, etc. External failure cost occurs when a company fails to produce good quality products after the product reaches the customer. Classified as external failure costs are complaint handling cost, warranty cost, product replacement cost, customer compensation cost, recall cost, and legal action cost, etc. (Gupta and Campbell, 1995).

Cost of quality costs might be fixed, but the companies must at least have cost of good quality higher than the cost of poor quality. This is important

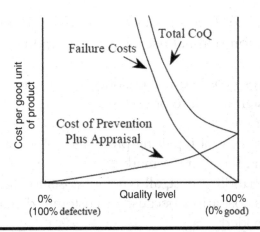

Figure 6.3   Comparison of cost of quality (Schiffauerova & Thomson, 2006).

because cost of poor quality, as we can see in Figure 6.1, can rise high and become uncontrollable. Figure 6.3 indicates a comparison between cost of good quality and cost of poor quality. It can be seen that ideally, over time, cost of poor quality (failure cost) decreases and cost of good quality (prevention and appraisal cost) increases.

The review above indicates that cost of poor quality is the cost that should be avoided whenever possible. Cost of poor-quality products are as follows (Oakland, 2003:26):

1. Internal failure cost
   a. Defective products cost, the occurring costs due to products that cannot be repaired, used, or sold.
   b. Shrinkage cost, incurring costs due to fluctuation in product expenditure. It may result in delays to the market.
   c. Rework or rectification cost, the cost for correcting poor material or mistakes to meet the requirements. The number of mistakes may increase employee's frustration and give an impact on working spirit.
   d. Downtime cost, the incurring costs when the production process is temporarily stopped.
   e. Re-inspection cost, cost of re-checking the rectified product or work.
   f. Downgrading cost, losses arising from the product sale that should be sold at a certain price, but it sold at a cheaper price (second quality) because it does not meet the specifications but still can be used.
   g. Waste cost, costs arising from conducting unnecessary work or storing inventory as a result of mistakes, poor management, wrong

material, extraordinary losses (e.g., due to natural disasters), normal losses, non-optimal use of supplies and equipment, long cycle period, etc.

   h. Failure analysis cost, cost of conducting activities that examine the causes of internal failure or service.

2. External failure cost

   a. Service cost, cost of repairing products that are already at customers' hand and those in the market.

   b. Complaint handling cost, all types of costs to handle customer complaints. This cost arises because of customer dissatisfaction with the product provided.

   c. Warranty cost, cost due to product replacement or repair that are still under warranty.

   d. Product replacement cost, cost due to product replacement in the market, for example expired prematurely.

   e. Returning cost, costs due to handling and investigation of rejected products, including transportation and expedition cost.

   f. Customer losses cost, incurring cost to replace losses received by customer of certain products.

   g. Liability cost, costs due to litigation of product liabilities and other claims violated by the company due to the relevant product, including contract changes cost, rescheduling cost, and changes in order cost.

   h. Product recall cost, costs arising because products have mass problems and are withdrawn entirely from the market.

   i. Bad will cost, cost arising as a result of damage to the reputation and image directly to the sales, including loss of customer.

   j. Legal action with customer, arising cost because the customers bring the case to the court.

Chapter 7

Lean Implementation

So, how to implement lean? Let us go back to the focus of lean. The focus of lean is culture, customer value, and focusing on process. Lean implementation does not start with lean culture. The definition of culture is "a pattern of shared basic assumptions that are learned as it solved problems that has worked well enough to be considered valid and, therefore, to be taught to new members as the correct way to perceive, think, and feel in relation to those problems". Therefore, lean culture is a culture that bases assumptions on lean in solving problems. This culture is established on success in conducting lean in the early stages. It is clear that for culture to exist, lean must exist at the first place. It is impossible to apply lean from lean culture because it is the lean culture which requires lean implementation.

Lean implementation starts from the second focus that is customer value. Customer value is not the initial requirement of lean. Instead, it is the basis for starting the lean process. To achieve customer value, relationships with customers is required. In other words, the first step to implement lean is *dealing with customers*.

Dealing with Customers

Establishing relationship with customer is the first step in implementing lean. It requires different additional approaches from business in general. Establishing relationship here does not mean that the company merely collects the requirements from customers. If this step is taken, then a general marketing survey requirement has to be met. However, establishing relationship with customer is more than that. It means building up the existing relationship to a higher level both in terms of intimacy and understanding (Middleton, Flaxel, & Cookson, 2005).

In marketing, there are two different concepts related to this problem. Establishing relationship with customer means introducing company to customers or vice versa, that is, introducing customers to the company. The first concept, introducing company to customers, is not the concept of establishing relationship with customer meant by lean (Verhoef & Leeflang, 2009). Introducing company to customer is only a form of general promotion activity. Here, marketers only actively introduce products to all society levels, expecting that they will be interested in the product and hence purchase it. This is called market orientation (Verhoef and Leeflang, 2009). Market orientation is the company action to actively monitor and understand customer and market needs.

Establishing relationship with customer as meant by lean is the role of marketing to represent customer, rather than representing the company. Here, marketers actively introduce customer to all levels within the company. This action strengthens the impact of marketing in the company. This impact must be maintained since the knowledge about customers' information may be lost. However, in fact, many companies fail to connect themselves with their customers in this way as they use market-orientated paradigm instead of building customer relationship (Verhoef and Leeflang, 2009).

To build customer relationship, the marketing division should emphasize on customer point of views. It works by translating the customer needs into customer solution, so that they become critical to the function of organization. Companies do not need to use various tricks to deceive customers for buying their products, instead they must provide valuable products to the customers (Verhoef and Leeflang, 2009).

The explanation above indicates that lean actually starts from the marketing line. Lean exists at the end of the process, not at the beginning of production process as we usually know. Marketing line is customer representative for the company. As a representative, it reports customer values to the company. Furthermore, as the company will start the lean process, the customer values are trusted for marketing for them to be delivered to the customers.

This situation raises doubt about the authority in a company (Russo-spena & Mele, n.d.). In general organization, products are manufactured according to the expectation and order of the superior. However, in lean organization, products are manufactured in accordance with the customer expectation and needs. Therefore, we can see an example of a democratic system. In a democratic system, people are the policy-makers. Even though there are presidents and regional heads, they are actually representatives of the people. Likewise, at the end, lean organization requires this process where the company leaders are the customer representatives. Thus, order and needs from the superior are in line with customer order and needs.

Shifting Focus to Process

After customer value is obtained, organization can focus on the process to reduce waste so that customer value is fulfilled. The organization which focuses on processes is run by humans and machines. Using this focus, the organization may ensure their results are meeting customer values and hence it can be repeated continuously. Directional views of three types of processes are as follows (Emiliani & Stec, 2004):

1. Value adding process: This process must be maintained because it fulfills the needs of customer as stated by the marketing division.
2. Non-adding value process but required: Process that does not add value but is needed. This process cannot be eliminated because it is the part of production process.
3. Waste: Waste is a process that does not add value and not needed in production. This process shall be removed. If this process is found, the team must work quickly to find the waste and immediately make improvement.

According to Emiliani and Stec (2004), the focus on process is caused by two issues: lean beliefs by the manager and simple business metrics. Belief is something accepted as truth. Emiliani and Stec (2004) conducted a study on two processes implementing lean, which were iron and steel brackets manufacturing and insurance policy-making. Tables 7.1 and 7.2 indicate old beliefs and lean beliefs in the process of iron and steel brackets manufacturing and insurance policy-making (Emiliani and Stec, 2004).

Those beliefs will lead to the focus on production because managers are encouraged to behave according to those beliefs. These behaviors are process-focused behaviors. Managers will visit shop and factory often, work with employees to discuss production issues, and blame process, not the people, if there is a mistake (Emiliani and Stec, 2004). There will be no time

Table 7.1   Old Belief and Lean Belief on Bracket Production Process

Old Belief	Lean Belief
Requires many processes, adding new steps if needed	Making a bracket with fewer processes
Requires two welding operations and two assembly operations	Welding and assembly operations can be combined
It takes two shifts to meet customers' demand	Currently, it requires two shifts but it might be down to one shift if there are new ideas
Production control determines what will be produced, how much to produce, and when to produce	Customer determines what will be produced, how much to produce, when to produce, and how to provide information using a simple *kanban* card
Requires long waiting time and cannot be reduced	Waiting time can be reduced
	Waste is on every process
Great works in process are needed to meet consumer demand	Do not need a lot of work in process to meet customer requirements
Inventory is an asset	Inventory is a waste
Stamping machine exchange time cannot be reduced	Stamping machine exchange time can be reduced
Cost per unit is reduced by increasing volume	A shorter exchange time will reduce cost per unit
Cannot change the shipping agreement of steel coil suppliers	Steel coil suppliers are valuable resources that can better meet our needs
Raw material cost is reduced by increasing the purchasing volume	Only purchase what is needed when it is needed
Processes does not need to be integrated; each process requires its own speed	Processes need to be integrated, for what the downstream process requires
I do not need to worry about what happened in the factory; someone has already taken care of it	I have to understand what happens in the company to help ensuring customer satisfaction

Source: Emiliani and Stec (2004).

Table 7.2   Old Beliefs and Lean Beliefs in Insurance Policy Making Process

Old Beliefs	Lean Beliefs
Many production steps are required; add new steps if needed	Make policies with fewer processes or combining the existing processes
Requires 59 workers; add employees if needed	Job content determines staff needs
Single-skilled employees are more efficient	Multi-skilled employees are assets
Current level of individual process quality is quite good, especially if IGO (in good order) >90%	Maximize the employment
Department is responsible to determine schedules and priorities for each individual process	Customers determine the production level
	Scheduled process is in the order of first-in first-out at one point
Long waiting time and cannot be reduced	Waiting time can be reduced
No lost value when queuing	Waste is on each process
Automatization is more efficient	Production will be efficient if it flows continuously
Production in batches is more efficient to reach the economics of scale	Ideal lot size is 1
"Push" products produce more output	Quality is the top priority
Conduct quality inspection on the product	Quality is established through the process
	Simplicity is the key to low cost
The amount of individual process efficiency results in overall system efficiency	The local optimum number is not the same as the optimum system
	Controlled inventory will result in a stable waiting time
Process does not need to be integrated; each process requires its own pacie	Processes need to be integrated; produce only when requested by the downstream process

Source: Emiliani and Stec (2004).

for the managers to make assumptions about the occurring process because they can immediately see the reality in the field. There is no time for the managers to talk about other things except the process. Some of the discussed issues are counterproductive, such as organizational political problems or small talks outside the work context.

Focus on the process ensures that customers obtain appropriate products. This process will make customer feel satisfied. In the same time, companies also obtain benefits. Only by looking at the efficiency generated by lean process, companies are benefited by cost reduction. Moreover, another benefit is the satisfied customers who will become more loyal and recommend the products or services to their partners. Overall, this will lead to the company competitive advantages (El Shenawy, Baker, & Lemak, 2007).

Involving People

After beliefs and metrics are strengthened and built, the next step is involving the people in production process to generate lean process. From the beginning, where waste is identified, production people need to be involved. It is performed by making value stream map (VSM). It is impossible for the planner to always map the process when it occurs. The employees in the production level see and conduct the process, so their contribution is very important to produce an accurate VSM (El Gohary, 2005).

VSM does not have to be prepared by gathering all employees. The planner can map the processes physically by taking a tour around the factory through a step-by-step process. To be more convincing, the mapping must be done from the end to the beginning. The planner starts observing from the final step and moves backwards to the beginning of process (El Gohary, 2014). During the process, the planner can ask details of the steps taken and other matters to the relevant employees.

Alternatively, the planner can observe the whole process from one strategic place in the factory. The planners can go up and observe the production process from a top perspective. Afterwards, the planner visits each process to see the steps taken in detail.

The reverse mapping or atop mapping strategy, from the earlier explanation, depends on the factory layout, nature of the process, employees' physical location and inventory, flow speed, and other services provided

(El Gohary, 2014). In any mapping strategy, production employees need to be involved to obtain input that presents the value stream accurately (El Gohary, 2014). The map-makers are the parties who have a general description, while the specific description is in the hands of those who are directly involved in each step of the process.

The involvement of employees in finding solutions to waste problems is equally important. They need to be involved in discussion to find the problems and take corrective measures. This involvement will make them feel they are the part of the corrective action. This step motivates them, especially if the company shows support and encourages them to conduct these improvements. They will feel responsible to the process they developed together. This step has a double effect. First, it will eliminate waste because waste has become a problem and must be removed. Second, involvement will encourage employees to work better, so the quality and quantity of the process will increase (Ramadan, 2015).

Frid and Utterstrom (2014) add that involvement of employees who work closest to the process will bring another effect, that is, lean sustainability. It is achieved when the employees who work in the process continue to maintain their achievements. They are ready to be involved in the next opportunity. They will monitor the waste and immediately report it if there is an opportunity provided by the company. Through this way, the lean process will run sustainably.

On the higher level, employee involvement is required to integrate lean culture. Company needs to establish comprehensive communication programs to build lean culture (Bay, Tang, & Bennett, 2004). Through this program, the company provides reasons why lean needs to be applied in all parts of the organization (Bay et al., 2004). In addition, this program serves as a source of ongoing reinforcement for anyone committed to change to the lean culture. The communication program also plays a role in creating the same theme, so it will establish lean beliefs on the employee level. If lean beliefs are embedded on the level of managers and employees, then lean culture can be quickly absorbed by the organization.

Establishing Connection with Customers

The first step to implement lean is building relationship with customers. Traditionally, introducing companies to customers is only a form of common promoting activities. Establishing relationship with customers is the role of marketing department to represent customers, rather than representing the company. Many companies fail to connect with their customer because they use traditional paradigms instead of building customer relationship by lean (Verhoef & Leeflang, 2009).

According to Shah and Ward (2007), relationship with customers is characterized by a number of indicators, such as:

1. Companies often make close contact with customers
2. Customers provide feedback on service quality and performance
3. Customers are actively involved in current and future product offers
4. Customers are directly involved in current and future product offers
5. Customers often share information on current and future demand with the marketing department

We can take a concept of customer orientation in marketing service as a form of establishing relationship with customers. In the field of service, employees are trying to make customers feel special. Special means an important individual for the company. For service employees, they should build this relationship (Donavan et al, 2004). Service employees must be serious in establishing communication verbally and non-verbally with their customers. In other words, service employees must be able to read the customers. This reading process is related, at least, to understanding the customers on a personal level. The need for building personal relationship with customers is rarely conducted by goods companies, even though it is important for them to understand customer values (Donavan et al., 2004).

Financial service companies are even more aggressive in establishing relationship with customers. They have proposition of values and prepare their capabilities (Lim, 2009). They have a mechanism to detect personal life events to identify whether a person has common life events. When they find someone, they establish relationship with him/her, check whether he/she has common life events, and then offer financial solutions. Absolutely, this is a combination of market and customer orientation. They are looking for common life events, which they have known from market research related to customer behavior, life needs, and customer choices to meet those living needs (Lim, 2009).

Feedback

For lean companies, they do not offer anything new. Lean companies only track how customers respond to the products they use for a long time. If the company is an individual, feedback may be difficult to accept as it relates to its existence. However, company is a group of people. Feedback can become a new issue to make the company better. Customer feedback and input will help improve product quality to be better. Therefore, feedback is mutually beneficial.

A commonly used device to *track customer feedback* and input is relationship management (Tyagi, Varma, & Vidyarthi, 2013). This concept has some versions such as traditional relationship management, electronics relationship management, mobile relationship management, and social relationship management. Relationship management covers all activities involving customer, starting from the frontline (sales, marketing, and support) to the backline (finance, R&D, production, and human resource). The concept of relationship management was first developed in the mid-1990s (Hasani, Bojei, & Dehghantanha, 2017). This concept is developed from the relationship marketing which is more focused on the efforts to encourage customers' commitment and loyalty (Hasani et al., 2016).

The role of technology is very important in relationship management. As can be seen from the classification of relationship management previously, this classification is closely related to technology. Electronics relationship management is related to the Internet. Mobile relationship management is related to mobile technology. Social relationship management is related to social media technology such as Facebook, Instagram, YouTube, and Twitter (Hasani et al., 2016). Social media is the most recent type of relationship management (Hasani et al., 2016). Social media serves to encourage customer involvement in marketing campaign and reach the new business partners. In addition, for lean companies, social media serves as a device for customer feedback tracker.

After the lean company obtains feedback and input from the feedback tracking process, the lean company should make the feedback *available internally*. This is performed by circulating the feedback to the relevant employees in the process and the managers on duty. By this method, it is easier for them to adjust the process with the feedback.

Real Needs

The feedback is *customers' real needs*. If something is a need, then its fulfillment is valuable. So, it can be said that the lean process is catalytic. Catalytic means responding to the customers' real needs in time and directly. In time means directly taking the customers' feedback. Direct means converting the feedback into the specification that is adding value.

In line with this method, lean process is no longer using the old paradigm of glorifying *projections*. Projection is no longer feasible for lean. It no longer provides functionality for the company. For lean companies, there is no difference between the customer needs and company needs; instead, it is mutual cooperation between customers and company. The company eliminates its ego to provide as many products as possible and expects that customers are interested in their proposition. The company shifts the gravity center to customer needs so that the customers become the indicator of process and product output.

This real need goes into the production system through kanban mechanism. Kanban are cards, chutes, and electronic signals to make the production system respond only to the real needs, not as prediction (Dentz, Nahmens, & Mullens, 2009). This real need is in the final process. Kanban taken from the customer and then goes to the end of production. Furthermore, the end of production calls the product from the previous stage. This continues so that customers only obtain products when they need them, with valuable specification.

In short, it can be said that companies provide technology to accommodate feedback and marketing fields that are representing customer to express their needs and amounts to the company. Afterwards, feedback is taken and distributed to the internal company. The internal company then establishes a lean process to add value to old products so that the product has facilitated provided feedbacks. Furthermore, customers obtain these new products with better quality. Customers then experience the benefits and start ordering again. Production runs according to the real needs on customer side using kanban system. There is no prediction on what customer needs and how much the customer needs, both rely on real needs.

How do companies understand that their needs are real, not projection from managers or marketing? By using relationship management and marketing commitment as the voice for the customers. These two issues should be able to eliminate doubts regarding the needs and the number of customers' needs.

Focus on the Output

In this case, the company needs to *focus on the output*. This seems a contradiction. Did not we say earlier that lean focuses on processes, not on the output? Actually, if the lean process is already running, the process and the output must be the same because both are coming from the same needs. The focus on output here is making the output as a reference point. Isn't the customer receiving the final result (what) is not asking for the process (how)? How the product with that value is reached in the hand the lean process, while what the final product is in the customer hands after receiving it in the end of lean process. Customers do not dictate what processes should be used to produce their desired products. These processes are developed by the lean team in accordance with the expected output. When the processes are planned through VSM, the team focuses on the process. This shift in focus ensures that the output in the customer have added value and no waste in the process. Without focusing on the final results in the early stages of lean, the innovation cannot arise (Drewery, 2003). In fact, innovations are important to effectively eliminate waste.

Moreover, the opposite of focus on final product is not the focus on process, but *internal convenience*. The focus on final product is not different from focus on process because final process and product are a unity. However, it is different from internal comfort, because it means that company manufactures products according to their capacity. They do not want to work too hard to meet customer needs that one day increase to very high. Many companies prioritize internal convenience, so it closes the other stakeholder's access, including customers (Millman, Wilson, Stevensen, & Cooper, 1995).

Focus on output is the basis of lean criticism. Critics view lean=mean (Hardon, Montecinos, & Roberts, 2005). Meaning that, lean is cruel because it spurs employees to work according to the output determined by customers. If customers need particular complicated values and require them in large quantities, employees will try desperately to reach it. This process is even worse if employees cannot obtain additional human resources because of the belief that increasing the number of employees is a waste.

Indeed, the research indicates that high work intensity results in stress, dissatisfaction, hurting behavior, and poor health for employees (Anderson-Connolly, Grunberg, Greenberg, & Moore, 2002). However, in the same study, Anderson-Connolly et al. (2002) documented a number of lean positive effects. In fact, these positive effects outweigh the negative effects.

Table 7.3   Lean Effect on Employees' Welfare

Lean Components	Effect on Employees	Effect on Managers
Increasing work intensity	Increasing stress, reducing job satisfaction, increasing harmful behavior, reducing health	Increasing stress, reducing job satisfaction, increasing harmful behavior, reducing health
Increasing work autonomy	Reducing stress, increasing job satisfaction, reducing harmful behavior, improving health	Reducing stress, increasing job satisfaction, increasing harmful behavior, reducing health
Skills training and improvement	Increasing stress, reducing job satisfaction, increasing harmful behavior, reducing health	Increasing stress, increasing job satisfaction, increasing harmful behavior, improving health
Collaboration in teams	Reducing stress, reducing job satisfaction, reducing harmful behavior, reducing health	Reducing stress, reducing job satisfaction, reducing harmful behavior, improving health
Computerization	Reducing stress, increasing satisfaction, reducing harmful behavior, improving health	Reducing stress, reducing satisfaction, reducing harmful behavior, improving health

Source: Anderson-Connolly et al. (2002).

Table 7.3 summarizes the results of Anderson-Connolly et al.'s (2002) research of lean effect on a number of employees' welfare indicators.

All the elements in the table are more or less presented by lean process. However, since the focus is directed at customers' demand, the more the satisfied customers, the more the demand exist. If the employees' work capacity does not increase while there is no new employee addition, the work intensity will increase. However, employees are also given great autonomy. This autonomy comes from their involvement in decision-making regarding what steps to eliminate waste should be conducted. The company will not allow employees to work in the same capacity if the demand for goods increases. If the employee's addition is considered as a waste, the alternative is increasing employee's skills. Otherwise, employees will experience burnout and the company will suffer losses. Moreover, employees who have many skills are additional values because they have their optimum potential and no potential is wasted. Teamwork is also core of lean because it is human nature to help each other. Similarly, computerization is an important solution to eliminate waste.

When it is viewed comprehensively, lean results in reducing stress rather than increasing it. For employees and managers, stress increases as the work and training intensity increases. Meanwhile, stress decreases due to work autonomy, teamwork, and computerization. In lean context, work does not always increase especially if the work in process is wasteful or waste of inventory. Further, this is compensated by training. Training can increase stress because there is additional time in the factory to attend the education process. However, it is important to increase the employees' capacity. Moreover, higher skills mean great human resource value and it serves as an investment for the employee if one day they decide to leave the company.

The same issue is observed in ordinary employees on harmful behavior problems. They are more careful when work autonomy increases, they collaborate in teams, and work is computerized, but they become more careless when the work intensity is high and follow training. However, for managers, carelessness can occur more often. Managers more often show harmful behaviors due to high work intensity, increasing work autonomy, and skills-training improvement. Managers are more careful when working in teams and computerization of work is done.

Job satisfaction becomes a problem for lean process. Table 7.3 indicates that job dissatisfaction is triggered by three factors, while job satisfaction only comes from two factors. For ordinary employees, they are only satisfied by autonomy and computerization, while not satisfied by the intensity of work, training, and teamwork. For managers, they are satisfied by work autonomy and training, but not satisfied by the intensity, teamwork, and computerization.

Other problems come from work health. Ordinary employees experience a health degeneration due to high work intensity, training and improvement in skills, and teamwork. They experience increasing occupational health issues due to the autonomy and computerization. For managers, lean further improves work health because of training, teamwork, and computerization. Managers experience a decline in occupational health due to high work intensity and increasing work autonomy.

So, lean processes can be criticized based on Anderson-Connolly et al.'s (2002) research in terms of behavior which brings harms to managers, employees' and managers' job satisfaction, and employees' health. This is indeed an important note for lean process implementation. However, conceptually, if lean is conducted seriously, these issues will not happen. Note that harmful behavior is a waste or a potential waste because it can cause damage to both product and company property. Lean companies should develop standardized measures of work so that the frequency of these harmful behaviors decreases. Similarly, health problems are clearly a waste. Employees become unable to work optimally and lot of time and energy is wasted. Maintaining employee health becomes an absolute practice to ensure waste removing. Regarding the problem of employee job satisfaction, this step can also cause waste problems because dissatisfied employees will work suboptimally. Further, without any effort to improve employee satisfaction, it is necessary to prevent waste. The effort to increase satisfaction does not necessarily mean work intensity reduction, training reduction, or not involving employees in the team. It can be achieved in many other ways that do not result in waste. For example, by providing incentives, bonuses, and so on.

One source of job dissatisfaction comes from the effort of eliminating waste itself. A certain amount of labor can be seen as a waste, therefore the company will reduce number of employees at any time, when it is considered there is a waste of labor. Downsizing of employees can reduce job satisfaction for employees who cannot discipline themselves because they are threatened with termination when they are not working optimally. However, Kinnie, Hutchinson, and Purcell (1998) found a solution to this problem. They suggest four solutions:

1. Communicate with the employees. Good communication is expected to facilitate an understanding to all employees regarding why companies need to conduct discipline procedures, what criteria are assessed, changes in what responsibilities, and what long-term plans the company has. This step will encourage a commitment from employees to make changes.
2. Providing welfare support for both careless employees and under-disciplined employees. This welfare support can include career counseling or stress management intervention such as employee assistance program.
3. Providing opportunities for all employees to take part in training and develop new skills, so new ways of working can be found for both individual employees and work groups.
4. Adjusting the company performance management system.

Another criticism on lean, generally, is its exploitative nature and that it does not respect people rights since it puts pressure on employees to eliminate waste (Hines et al., 2006). However, it comes from a misunderstanding of lean principles. It is mentioned earlier that lean is not a mechanical tool or technique. Lean is a combination of human and machine factors. It involves giving motivation to employees to work smartly, not hardly. Employees are empowered and valued, not left to become dairy cows and not cared for. These issues are important for lean because lean strives to be sustainable. If you want to be sustainable, then human factors must be maintained and well-nurtured physically and spiritually.

Loss of Sight on Customers and Their Needs

It is possible to *lose sight on customers and their needs*. Two forms of business initiatives, namely, time-to-market (TTM) and product recycling, result in a loss of view on customers (Hauser, 2000). TTM is a strategy to manufacture products quickly for sale on the market. The main goal is reducing cycle times as short as possible. TTM is not focused on customers but suppliers. The company establishes very good relationship with suppliers so that suppliers can provide raw materials as quickly as possible to meet company's large needs. Employees are encouraged to develop efficient product design methods, rapid manufacturing design ability, coordinate with each other effectively, and design products that facilitate the new technology integration.

Cycle time is one of the lean targets. Long cycle is certainly a waste, because it means the product goes through a long process and therefore customers need a long time to obtain the product. However, it can make a company lose sight on customers. A fast cycle time only works if there are many requests from customers. If the customers do not demand or the produced product does not have what the customers expect, the running process becomes futile. TTM process will only result in waste of inventory because produced goods cannot be absorbed by the market quickly and properly.

Product recycling strategies can also be problematic. Product recycling is reusing of old product features on new products, for example, in general design or some product parts. The objective is saving time in product design. Further, this process can result in a loss of focus on customers. A good product from a lean perspective is not a slightly different product from the old product. Indeed, the entire product should be recreated.

All processes depend on the customers. If the company focuses too much on recycling the products, the company can insist that certain product designs or parts must be retained even if they are not valuable according to customers.

Another strategy that can result in losing sight of customers is an effort to pursue maturity level in capability maturity model integration (CMMI) model (Glazer, Dalton, Anderson, Konrad, & Shrum, 2008). CMMI is one of the organization management and development frameworks. CMMI consists of five levels (Patel & Ramachandran, 2009):

1. Initial: In this level, the product process is ad hoc and sometimes chaotic. In this level, there are only a few clear processes and success depends on individual effort and heroism.
2. Repeatable: A basic project management process or plan is available to track costs, schedules, and functionality. The necessary discipline process is available to repeat the initial success of a new product with the same function.
3. Defined: The process for both management activities and techniques has been documented, standardized, and integrated into a standard production process for organizations. All products use a standardized version of approved process adapted to develop and maintain the product.
4. Managed: Detailed process indicators and product quality have been collected. Both the process and the product are quantitatively understood and controlled.
5. Optimizing: Continuous improvement process is possible with quantitative feedback from the process and piloting innovative ideas and technologies.

As can be seen from these levels, the word "customers" is never mentioned. It occurs because CMMI is not customer oriented. Indeed, there is a feedback and continuous improvement. However, this is directed from the process and product testing, not from the customers' needs and values. Companies that pursue positions in CMMI level are constrained by looking inward. Innovation exists but piloted by developing ideas from various sources, not necessarily from customers. Often, ideas are developed from entrepreneur's experience or customer's experience, and they come from quantitative, not qualitative market surveys. CMMI is a good example of process focus which is non-oriented to customer. Lean is process focus by adhering to customers' orientation.

The product development strategy is another example of a strategy that is risking losing sight on customers. Product development generally rests on the assumption that company understands its customers well. It is better to attract more money from the existing customers than obtaining difficult and more expensive customers in an intense competition (Wanjiku, 2010). Further, it occurs because they already understand the customer well, the company only needs to develop additional products to meet the customers' needs (Wanjiku, 2010), but product development can be problematic if the company only feels familiar with customers without evidence from the market research. The company finally developed a product that is believed to be able to meet customers' needs even though in reality the customers do not need it.

In general, companies will lose sight on customers if they are oriented inward, whether it is in the process, supplier, or product. CMMI is process oriented, not customer oriented. TTM and recycling strategy are efforts to reduce waste. TTM reduces cycle time while recycling strategies reduce design time and product errors/failures. Still, both are not customer oriented. The product development strategy is product oriented and likely to ignore waste because what it pursues is a new highly demanded product by the market.

Chapter 8

Focus on Process

As we discussed earlier, the focus on process is affected by two issues: simple business beliefs and metrics (Emiliani & Stec, 2004). Belief directs the attention of all organization members to the process, not to other issues such as political power in the factory or wasting time on other issues. Simple metrics allow a clear data collection from the process, so the decisions taken are accurate. This process will result in the improvement of running process if it is conducted continuously.

Lean Beliefs and Competencies

A list of lean beliefs has been discussed earlier. In this unit, we will view how these beliefs might lead to the process focus. According to Emiliani and Stec (2004), beliefs can lead to a process focus because beliefs lead to behavior. Behavior is an action based on belief. This behavior in turn leads to competence, which is the developing ability or capability because of that behavior. Competence will improve behavior to be better. Meaning, there is an interaction between behavior and competence. Behavior makes the focus on the current process running well, while competence makes the focus on the process runs not only in the present but also in the future.

Table 8.1 indicates the competencies generated by old beliefs in the bracket production process. Table 8.2 compares the competencies generated by lean beliefs in the same process (). Tables 8.3 and 8.4 do the same for the insurance policy-making process.

Table 8.1 Old Beliefs and Non-Lean Competencies on Bracket Production

Old Beliefs	Non-Lean Competencies
Needs many processes, adding new steps if needed	Maintain the status quo; increase costs (HR, materials, space, and equipment expenditures as well as future liabilities, such as pensions and health services) Increase waiting time
Needs two welding operations and two assembly operations	Maintain the status quo Employ more people than is really needed (excessive employees) Increase costs (HR, materials, space, and equipment expenditures and future liabilities, such as pensions and health services)
Takes two shifts to meet customers' demand	Maintain the status quo Excessive employees Increase costs (HR, materials, space, and equipment expenditures and future liabilities, such as pensions and health services)
Production control determines what will be produced, how much is produced, and when to produce	Cause confusion over what must be produced, how much is produced, and when to produce Increase costs (e.g., using software to calculate requirements) Create a need to continue to respond to the problems Provide incentives to people who are good in responding the problems
Long waiting time is needed and cannot be reduced	Maintain the status quo Not responsive to customers' needs changes Work in process management and final goods inventory
A large amount of work in process is needed to meet customers' demand	Overproduction Work in process management and final goods inventory
Inventory is an asset	Increasing costs (space and equipment needed to manage inventory)
Stamping machine exchange time cannot be reduced	Maintain the status quo Overproduction Increasing costs

(Continued)

Table 8.1 (*Continued*) Old Beliefs and Non-Lean Competencies on Bracket Production

Old Beliefs	Non-Lean Competencies
Cost per unit is reduced by increasing volume	Slow response on customers' demand changes (volume and mix)
Cannot change the shipping agreement of steel coil suppliers	
Raw material cost per unit is reduced by increasing the purchasing volume	Increasing costs (raw materials and overhead) Raw material inventories management
Processes do not need to be integrated; each process requires its own speed	Raw materials management, work in progress, and final goods inventory Slow response on customers' demand changes
I do not need to worry about what happens at the factory; someone has taken care of it	Do not understand adding-value and adding-waste processes Bad observation skills Focus on people/employees, not on the process

Source: Emiliani and Stec (2004).

Table 8.2 New Beliefs and Lean Competencies on Bracket Production

Lean Beliefs	Lean Competencies
Make a bracket with fewer processes	Challenging the status quo Cost reduction (HR, materials, space, and equipment expenditure and future liabilities, such as pensions and health services) Waiting time reduction
Welding and assembly operations can be combined	Challenging the status quo Employing employees not more than needed Cost reduction (human resources, materials, space, and equipment expenditure and future liabilities, such as pensions and health services)
Currently requires two shifts but it might be one shift if there are new ideas	Challenging the status quo Employ/place employees carefully for other adding-value activities Reducing costs (HR, materials, space, and equipment expenditures and future liabilities, such as pensions and health services)

(Continued)

Table 8.2 (*Continued*)   New Beliefs and Lean Competencies on Bracket Production

Lean Beliefs	Lean Competencies
Customers determine what will be produced, how much to produce, when to produce, and how to provide the information using a simple kanban card	Clarify what was been produced, how to produce, and when to produce Cost reduction (e.g., no need to buy software for daily work) Expedition reduction or elimination Giving rewards to employees who are great in improving the process
Waiting time can be reduced	Challenging the status quo Responsive on customers' demand changes
Waste is in every process	Waste identification and elimination Time-based competitiveness
Do not need a lot of work in process to meet customer requirements	Understand customer needs
Inventory is waste	Cost reduction (less inventory; less space and equipment to manage inventory)
Stamping machine time exchange can be reduced	Challenging the status quo Produce customers' demand Cost reduction
A shorter exchange time will reduce cost per unit	Quick response on customers' demand changes (volume and mix)
Steel coil suppliers are valuable resources that can make our needs better	Building relationship with suppliers
Only buy what is needed and when it is needed	Cost reduction (raw materials and overhead)
Processes need to be integrated, for what the downstream process requires	Material and information flow alignment Quick response on customers' demand changes
I have to understand what happens in the company to help ensuring customers' satisfaction	Understanding adding-value and adding waste processes Strong observing skills Focus on the process, not the person

Source: Emiliani and Stec (2004).

Table 8.3   Old Beliefs and Non-Lean Competencies on Insurance

Old Beliefs	Lean Competencies
Needs many production steps; add new steps if needed	Maintaining the status quo Increasing costs (HR, materials, space, and equipment expenditures as well as future liabilities, such as pensions and health services) Increasing waiting time
Fifty-nine workers are needed; add employees if needed	Maintaining the status quo Employing more people than really needed (excessive employees) Increasing costs (HR, materials, space, and equipment expenditures and future liabilities, such as pensions and health services)
Single-skilled workers are more efficient	Give awards to specialists
Quality level of individual process is quite good, especially if IGO (in good order)>90%	Maintaining the status quo Encouraging and rewarding local optimization
Department is responsible for determining schedules and priorities for each individual process	Causing confusion over what must be produced, how much is produced, and when to produce Creating a continuous expedition Incentivizing good people in responding to problems
Long waiting time is needed and cannot be reduced	Maintaining the status quo
There is no value lost when queuing	Not responsive on customers' demand changes
Automation is more efficient	Overproduction Increasing costs and complexity
Production in batches is more efficient by reaching scale economy	Overproduction Increasing costs (raw materials and overhead) Buying and making large quantities
Product "push" yields more output	Overproduction Increasing costs (raw materials and overhead)
Conduct quality inspection on the product	Increasing cost and complexity Providing incentive to good people in responding on their repeat problems

(Continued)

Table 8.3 (*Continued*) Old Beliefs and Non-Lean Competencies on Insurance

Old Beliefs	Lean Competencies
	Giving rewards for dysfunctional behaviors Encouraging local optimization
Processes do not need to be integrated; each process requires its own pace	Overproduction Increasing cost and complexity

Source: Emiliani and Stec (2004).

Table 8.4 New Beliefs and Lean Competences on Insurance

Lean Beliefs	Lean Competences
Can make the policies with fewer processes or existing processes can be combined	Challenging the status quo Cost reduction (HR, materials, space, and equipment expenditure and future liabilities, such as pensions and health services) Waiting time reduction
Job content determines staff needs	Challenging the status quo Employing employees not more than what is needed Cost reduction (human resources, materials, space, and equipment expenditure and future liabilities, such as pensions and health services)
Employees with multiple skills are assets	Challenging the status quo Employing/placing employees carefully for other adding-value activities
Maximize the use of employees	Cost reduction (human resources, materials, space, and equipment expenditure and also future liabilities, such as pensions and health services)
Customers determine production level	Clarifying what is produced, how much is the production, and when to produce
Scheduled process is in the order of first-in first-out at one point	Reducing costs (e.g., deleting a number of schedule points and expeditions) Providing incentives to people who are good in improving the process
Waiting time can be reduced	Challenging the status quo Responsive on customers' demand changes

(*Continued*)

Table 8.4 (*Continued*) New Beliefs and Lean Competences on Insurance

Lean Beliefs	Lean Competences
Waste is in every process	Time-based competitiveness Waste identification and elimination
Production will be efficient if it flows continuously	Challenging the status quo Producing and responding on customers' demand (volume and mix)
Ideal lot size is 1	Developing sight on flow
Quality is top priority	Root problem analysis
Quality is established through the process	Cost reduction (e.g., variation reduction) Anti-error
Simplicity is key on low cost	Challenging the status quo Cost reduction (human resource expenditure, materials, space and equipment) Overhead reduction
Local optimum number is not the same as the optimum system	Organization adjustment Thinking as a system
Controlled inventory will result in a stable waiting time	Cost reduction (inventory and material management) Waiting time reduction and stabilization
Processes need to be integrated; produce only when demanded by the downstream process	Align the material and information flow Clear information flow (without deviation)

Source: Emiliani and Stec (2004).

Simple Business Metrics

The discussed beliefs and competencies focus on the process, but they are not sustainable because the end points of process focus have not been clearly defined. To clarify the process end points, a metric is needed. Metrics are indicators of process quality. Metrics must be simple, in the sense that they can be measured by anyone at that moment. Absolutely, this metric must be calculated without tools. It can be seen directly or only needs simple mathematics such as plus, minus, times, and divides. These indicators are actually subjective, depending on the result of value stream mapping (VSM). However, we can see in the examples from Emiliani and Stec (2004), the metrics used to stream bracket creation value such as the following:

1. What are customers' demands and when they are produced and how much?
2. What is the coming supply and how much?
3. Machine exchange time
4. Produced bracket quantity
5. Engine average uptime
6. System waiting time
7. Processing time

The metrics of insurance policy production used are as follows:

1. Number of workers
2. Achieved output in the first process
3. Information system average uptime
4. Policy demand level (takt time)
5. System waiting time
6. Maximum processing time

Note that the metrics above do not focus on one step but on the whole step. This is important because if it is only directed at one step, there will be a desire to optimize the local process. This effort can result in other metric changes, which may result in conflicts between local management people and the whole process people (Emiliani and Stec, 2004).

Focus on process is further operationalized to reduce waste. Simple metrics are applied on today's VSM. The team holds discussions to find the root of problem and how to resolve it. These roots and steps are based on existing beliefs and competences. Further, a future VSM is prepared as the ideal target of improvement process. Figure 8.1 exemplifies two simple VSMs. The left VSM indicates current VSM and the right VSM indicates the future VSM.

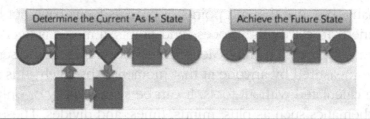

Figure 8.1   Current and future VSM.

Chapter 9

Involving the People

Involving employees in lean processes is a crucial step. The process of identifying and eliminating waste must involve employees. It is necessary for two reasons (Boehm, 2005). First, they are stakeholders who are critical to the success, so they need to be represented. Second, they have expertise in determining feasible solutions. In fact, failure to involve employees in finding solutions to the problems is seen as one of the HR waste root causes (Ray, Ripley, & Neal, 2006).

Employees in the production level are those who see and conduct the process; hence, their contribution is very important to produce accurate value stream mapping (VSM). During the VSM process, the planner can ask for details of the steps taken and other matters to the person in charge. In any mapping strategy, production employees need to be involved to obtain an accurate input which presents the value stream. The employees will be involved by providing status report. This status report is used as a comparison to goal performance, so that appropriate corrective actions can be taken if needed (Sacks, Radosavljevic, & Barak, 2010). Map-makers are the parties who have a general overview, whereas the specific view is in the hands of those directly involved in each process step.

The employee involvement in the phase of finding solutions on waste is equally important. Sometimes, managers make bad decisions. Engaging employees affected by these decisions and working alongside them to find the best solutions has proven as an effective step in correcting manager's mistakes (Lindhard & Wandahl, 2012).

This step has motivated them. Especially, if the company supports and encourages them to conduct these improvements. The employee engagement step will eliminate waste as a problem and the waste is committed to be removed. In addition, involvement encourages employees to work better, so the process quality and quantity increases. The involvement of employees who work closest to the process will have another effect, namely, lean sustainability. Lean sustainability is achieved because employees continue to maintain their achievements. In this way, the lean process becomes sustainable.

In the higher level, employees' involvement is needed to integrate lean culture. The company needs to build a comprehensive communication program to build a lean culture. In addition, this program serves as a source of ongoing reinforcement for anyone committed to change to a lean culture. The communication program also plays a role in creating the same theme over and over again to build lean beliefs at the employee level.

Basically, change will not only happen by designing a better process. There are human factors in the process and these factors need to be considered. The company should involve the relevant people to work in the repair process. Make it clear why they must be involved and make it easier for them to adopt and adapt to the new ways of conducting the production process.

Overall, human problems in lean organization are under the theme of organization obstacles. Organization obstacles are various problems originating from a group of people who are in the system or related to lean systems. A number of organization obstacles identified in lean process implementation may differ depending on the organization. Organization obstacles on lean implementation in the public sector include the following (Radnor & Walley, 2008):

1. Poor focus on clear customer
2. People work in isolated environment
3. Too many targets
4. Lack of awareness and strategic guidance
5. Lack of understanding on impact of variation, system thinking, and process flow

Čiarnienė and Vienažindienė (2013) present the types of obstacles in lean implementation based on human obstacles and organization obstacles as indicated in Table 9.1.

Shang and Pheng (2014) in their research on contracting companies in China identified six barriers on lean implementation:

1. People and partner barrier
   a. High labor turnover
   b. High tolerance for uncluttered workspaces
   c. Absence of lean culture in business partners
   d. Insufficient lean knowledge
   e. Insufficient delivery performance
   f. Multi-layer subcontractor
2. Managerial and organizational barrier
   a. Limited use of off-site construction techniques
   b. Avoid decision-making and responsibility
   c. Hierarchy in organizational structure
   d. Insufficient management skills
   e. Use of amicable resolution to cover mistakes
   f. Lack of empowerment

Table 9.1 Main Obstacles in Lean Implementation

Obstacles Type		Evidences
Related to human	Resistance on change	Lean production implementation sometimes requires significant changes in organization attitudes, which can be very challenging if the organization is not ready for the change
	Perception and lack of knowledge	Lack of understanding on lean knowledge, principles, and techniques for managers and employees
	Improvement in team identity	Often consists of people who are willing to be involved rather than people who must be involved
	Poor communication	Use of excessive jargon and lack of clear messages for staff

(Continued)

Table 9.1 (*Continued*)   Main Obstacles in Lean Implementation

Obstacles Type		Evidences
Related to organization	Compartmentalization	Fragmentation into functional and professional silos provides main and functional obstacles constraints for flow of customers, goods, and information
	Hierarchy and cultural issues	Based on the staff hierarchy and the way management roles are allocated, it usually becomes an obstacle to any improvement
	High implementation costs and lack of resources	Lean implementation sometimes means removing completely the previous setup and system of a physical installation; efficient machine purchasing and employee training can increase company expenses
	Poor relationships between improvement programs and strategies	Lean improvement programs are not included in company strategies
	Data collection and performance measurement	It is necessary to indicate progress and assess the effectiveness of various implemented changes, tools, and techniques

Source: Čiarnienė and Vienažindienė (2013).

3. Lack of support and commitment
   a. Resistance to management changes
   b. Resistance to employee changes
   c. Inadequate training
4. Cultural and philosophical barrier
   a. Lack of long-term philosophy

    b. Absence of lean culture in the company

    c. Lack of support from top management

5. Barrier related to the government

    a. Strict requirements and agreements

    b. Lack of support from the government

6. Barrier related to procurement

    a. Limited involvement of construction companies on design

    b. Limited use of design and build procurement modes

Sheng and Pheng (2014) recommended a number of improvements to overcome the barriers.

Table 9.2 presents some of the alternative solutions for each of existing problems.

Table 9.2　Solution to Lean Implementation Barrier

Barrier	Solutions
1. People and partner barrier	
a. High labor turnover	Providing competitive salaries for frontline employees
b. High tolerance for uncluttered workspaces	Companies must emphasize on workspace cleanliness policies aligned with training Training is directed at the 5S method and best practices for the workplace
c. Absence of lean culture in business partners	Cooperation must be sought to grow alongside the partners; partners must be aware that they are part of the company, so that mutual trust can be established into cooperation foundation to improve joint performance
d. Insufficient lean knowledge	Training involving lean practice concepts and methods, waste standardization and elimination, etc.
e. Insufficient delivery performance	Partnership development with subcontractors who only have labor for sustainable labor supply
f. Multi-layer subcontractor	Government needs to be aware of limiting multi-layer subcontracting systems, so contractors can observe lower-level subcontractors and understand their concern and problems more efficiently to solve the problems quickly

(Continued)

Table 9.2 (*Continued*)   Solution to Lean Implementation Barrier

Barrier	Solutions
2. Managerial and organizational barrier	
a. Limited use of off-site construction techniques	Top management must appreciate the benefits of off-site techniques and adopting them
b. Avoid decision-making and responsibility	Developing management skills and capabilities, including leadership, mentoring, willingness to take responsibility, proactive decision-making, establishing trust with employees, etc.
c. Hierarchy in organization structure	
d. Insufficient management skills	
e. Use of amicable resolution to cover mistakes	
f. Lack of empowerment	Establishing mutual trust between managers and employees with a good empowerment in certain fields such as quality control, problem-solving, advice-giving schemes, etc.
3. Lack of support and commitment	
a. Resistance to management changes	Provide an explanation of changes to management and employees so that they can understand and feel motivated to adopt lean
b. Resistance to employee changes	
c. Insufficient training	Increasing the knowledge of frontline employees and other employees about lean through training in possible times such as on rainy days or evenings
4. Cultural and philosophical barrier	
a. Lack of long-term philosophy	Redesigning organizational culture or shifting organization culture
b. Absence of lean culture in the company	
c. Lack of support from top management	

(Continued)

Table 9.2 (*Continued*)   Solution to Lean Implementation Barrier

Barrier	*Solutions*
5. Barrier related to the government	
a. Strict requirements and agreements	Study recommendations and lean implementation success on the government level such as UK (Construction Task Force, 1998) or Singapore cases to set targets, prioritize lean on national agenda, and provide clear direction for construction companies to run lean
b. Lack of support from the government	
6. Barrier related to procurements	
a. Limited involvement of construction companies on design	Contractors and other stakeholders need to be encouraged to be involved in the design stages to promote collaboration and establish collaboration culture while provide feedback to prevent mistakes that may arise from design
b. Limited use of design and build procurements mode	

Source: Shang and Pheng (2014).

Chapter 10

Lean Principles

Principles are fundamental issues in distinguishing one process or mechanism from another. There are many opinions about what lean principles are. Liker (Höök, 2008) suggested four sections of lean. Each section has its own principles. We can see the sections and principles in Table 10.1.

If we look at the table, we can see that Liker views lean as four: philosophy, process, HR development, and problem-solving. Philosophy is the highest and abstract aspect, HR is the capital of organization to achieve the philosophy, process is the location where philosophy is embedded, and problem-solving is an effort to make the process sustainable. Indeed, philosophy is in the top of lean, but what about the position of each aspect?

Table 10.1 Lean Principles according to Liker

Section	Principles
Long-term philosophy	Determine management decisions based on long-term philosophy, even sacrifice the short-term financial goals
Right process will bring the right results	Create a continuous process flow to bring problems to the surface, use the pull system to avoid overproduction, lift workloads, and establish a culture of stopping to solve problems to obtain quality from the first time. Standardized tasks and processes are the fundamental of continuous improvement and employee empowerment, use visual controls so there are no hidden problems, and use only fully tested and reliable technology for your employees and processes.

(Continued)

Table 10.1 (*Continued*) Lean Principles according to Liker

Section	Principles
Add value to the organization by developing employees	Grow a leader who understands work as a whole and life philosophy, teaches others, develops extraordinary people and teams who follow the company's philosophy, and appreciates partners and supplier networks by challenging them and helping them to develop
Continuous root problem-solving encourages organization learning	Go and see for yourself to understand the whole situation, take decisions slowly based on consensus, fully considering the various choices; implement decisions quickly, and become a learning organization through continuous reflection and continuous improvement

Source: Höök (2008:33).

Lean principle classification is generally accepted as process oriented. It is a group of principles introduced by Womack and Jones. These principles are cyclical in the sense that they will return to the beginning after final part has been reached. Further, lean emphasizes on the process. In fact, Damrath (2012) observes that lean principles have their own strength because it is a series of steps to instill lean thinking. Lean principles are process-oriented, meaning to sort out the principles based on the process of lean implementation. This method is clearer and more structured. We understand that lean starts from identifying customer values, then mapping the process, and so on. Therefore, lean principles should also follow this process.

These lean principles, which are based on process, include the following (Jansson, Soderholm, & Johnsson, 2009):

1. Value
   a. Determine the customers
   b. Determine what is valuable for the customers
   c. Determine what is valuable for the executing team
   d. Determine how the value is specified by the products
2. Value stream
   a. Determine all production resources
   b. Determine all production activities required

    c. Standardize the current practice

    d. Determine and find position of key component suppliers

3. Stream

    a. Determine the non-adding value activities (waste)

    b. Discard or reduce the identified waste effect

    c. Identify the key performance indicators

    d. Measure the performance

4. Pull

    a. Keep the production system flexible on customers' demand

    b. Keep the production system to adapt on customers' future demand

    c. Be aware to reduce waiting time and cycle time

    d. Work until the last moment under the company responsibility.

5. Perfection

    a. Keep the production system transparent for all involved stakeholders

    b. Capture and implement experiences from completed projects

    c. Be aware to increase customer value

    d. Be aware to improve work implementation

Note that the principles above are strictly bound on lean stages, starting from identifying customers to work on implementation increasing on an ongoing basis. In this way, it is easy to trace whether lean principles have been obeyed or not within a process. Moreover, it is also easy to build evaluation criteria to consider whether a process can be said as a lean process or not. Table 10.2 indicates lean principles evaluation model.

It does not mean that philosophical principles, processes, HR development, and problem-solving are not important lean principles, but they are in another dimension. The process-based lean principles can be said as horizontal principles since they are sequential, while hierarchical-based principles can be said to be vertical principles. The process-based lean principles can be put in the position of process principle in the hierarchical-based principles. More specifically, we can see the two types of principles in Figure 10.1.

Figure 10.1 indicates that process-based principle lies in the second part of hierarchical principle. This principle replaces the principle in hierarchical lean principles process (Table 10.2). We can replace all principles in Table 10.1 with five lean processes that construct process-based principles in Table 10.2. Moreover, the principles in process are included in Table 10.2. Note that the creation of a continuous process flow to bring problems on surface is a part of waste identification (stream principle). Similarly, the

Table 10.2   Lean Evaluation Model Based on Lean Five Principles

Principle	Characteristic	Evaluation Criteria
Value	Identify values from the customer's point of view	Are customers known? Are customers value known? Is executing team's value known? How is the value transparency in information and images?
Value stream	Understand the value stream where values are delivered for the whole process	Are all the resources for the process known? Are all activities in the process known? Is the process standardized? Is the key information supplier known?
Stream	Reach a harmonic stream in the work process as waste is eliminated	Is the non-adding value activity (waste) known? Has the waste effect been removed or reduced? Is key performance indicator known? Is the performance measurable?
Pull	Reach an attraction, so there is no provided information until it is needed	Is the system flexible on customer demands? Can the system adapt to customers' demand in the future? Are there any efforts to shorten the delivery time and cycle? Is the work done in the last moment is still a part of the responsibility?
Improvement	Recognize that improvement must be pursued continuously	Are the system and routine transparent for all stakeholders? Is the experience from completed project taken and implemented? Is there any effort to improve value for customers? Is there any effort to improve work implementation?

Source: Jansson et al. (2009).

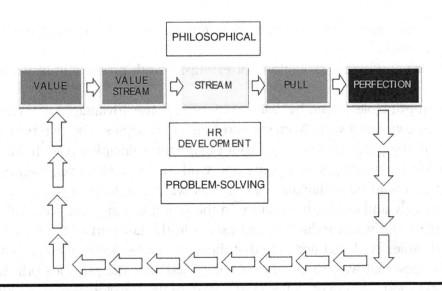

Figure 10.1   Two groups of lean principles.

principle of "using the pull system to avoid overproduction" is a part of activity in pull principle. Lifting workloads and stopping culture to solve problems are also part of pull system. Standardized tasks and processes are part of stream principle. Visual control is part of waste identification. The use of technology is part of waste elimination (stream principle). Therefore, it is allowed to eliminate all principles in the process and replace them with process-based principles.

Furthermore, the cyclical nature of value-based principle can be observed in Figure 10.1. The arrow that is returning from perfection to value indicates that lean principle is running cyclically in the process. In this cyclical process, HR development activities, skills sharpening, and problem-solving are conducted, which also facilitates hierarchical-based principles.

Adler, Hakkert, Kornbluth, and Hakkert (2012) suggest five lean principles that are basically only a modification of Womack and Jones's five lean principles. The five lean principles from Adler et al. (2012) are as follows:

1. Customer value identification, for example, a higher level of service for customers
2. Value stream management, for example, concentrating on quality products
3. Production value capability development, for example, technology improvement

4. Pull mechanism, for example, determining products' amount and distribution
5. Waste and excess reduction, for example, work protocol improvement

The lean principles given by Adler et al. have some advantages and disadvantages compared with Womack and Jones's principles. The five principles eliminate the perfection process, so it breaks the principle cycle chain. This is suitable for running lean in only one work process. However, we know that lean should be sustainable. We do not want lean to only run once but continuously and establish a culture in the organization. Moreover, Adler et al. place the waste reduction and excess in the last part of the principle. Indeed, Adler et al. did not state that these principles are sequential but they suggest that waste reduction is conducted after the previous principles are conducted. Moreover, Adler et al. separate the development of production flow capability with waste and excess reduction. They consider that technology improvement is not a part of waste and excess reduction. This type of thinking seems to come from an old paradigm that a process must be refined first before it is corrected. It means wasteful processes are conducted, and then waste is reduced. Obviously, this is impractical and definitively, paradoxical, because it results in waste of managerial action that seeks to eliminate waste.

Before explaining each principle, we should clarify the terms first. The terms of lean principles from Womack and Jones are often criticized for not providing a clear concept definition (Hopp & Spearman, 2004). Hopp and Spearman (2004) state that lean principles from Womack and Jones are the principles in tactical level, which is how to run lean, whereas Ohno states that at the strategical level. Womack and Jones proposed the concept of "pull" as "no one should produce goods or services until the downstream customers demand it" (Hopp and Spearman, 2004). It makes no sense, for example, a cashier in a supermarket waits for a customer to ask for a certain item, then supplies it. This is somewhat correct. Therefore, we see that "pull" concept in lean principles is not a tactical concept but a strategical concept. "Pull" means "focus on customer demand, 'not' providing the product after the customer asks" as understood by Womack and Jones.

Spear and Bowen (1999) even completely abandoned Womack and Jones's lean principles. They self-formulated lean principles based on direct observation in 33 Toyota factories. These observations produced four rules obeyed by all employees in running lean in Toyota. The four rules are as follows:

1. All work must be highly specified in terms of load, sequence, time, and output.
2. Every relationship between customers and suppliers must be direct and unambiguous when ordering and receiving responses.
3. Lines for each product and service must be simple and direct.
4. Any improvement must be made according to the scientific method, with guidance of a teacher, in the lowest possible level in organization.

From the four lean characteristics, Staats, James, and Upton (2011) succeeded in formulating four lean principles. The four lean principles according to Staats et al. are as follows:

1. Task specifications: tasks are specified for two main reasons:
   a. Specifications allow a continuous hypothesis test. Immediately after a task is specified based on substance, sequence, time, and output, two hypotheses can be tested each time the work is completed:
      - Is someone who completes the task is able to do it?
      - Will the activity produce quality output?
      - If one of these hypotheses is denied, the problem-solving cycle runs.

   b. When the work is specified and the actual conditions are compared with the expected conditions after the work is completed, the opportunity to make improvements increases.

2. Smooth communication: it is not only reducing complexity but also allowing team members to verify the significance of each step in the process and minimize total relationship, so the information can flow smoothly from customers to suppliers.
3. Simple process architecture: it is the relationship that constitutes the flow of goods, services, or information in the organization. Since communication runs smoothly, the process architecture must also be made simple and can diagnose itself.
4. Hypothesis-based problem-solving: Problem-solving must be conducted in the lowest possible level and involves testing hypotheses to push the organization to become ideal.

Lean principles from Staats et al. (2011) are scientific because they are drawn through careful scientific study. However, these principles do not indicate lean steps. These principles are also inherently included in Womack and Jones's principles. Task specification is a part of value stream, smooth communication is part of the stream, simple process architecture is part of the stream, while problem-solving is part of value stream. Therefore, let us focus on Womack and Jones by being careful and avoiding misunderstanding by holding on to the opinions of scientific circles.

Chapter 11

How to Define Values

Let us start from the first principle: value. More precisely, how to determine value. By knowing the value, a company can map the process and remove non-adding steps and only consume resources. What is value? There are several meanings of value (Salman, 2017):

1. Value is low cost
2. Value is anything needed in a product
3. Value is the quality obtained from paid cost
4. Value is what is obtained for what is given

For lean, value is all feasible activities in the view of customers (Ehsanifar & Rubin, 2011). Feasible here means caring for customers, so that external customers are willing to pay for it. The issues that customers care about are related to their needs, ability to pay, and time for their needs. Therefore, what is valuable to customers is what meets their needs in a certain price and time (Salman, 2017).

The term customers include internal customers and external customers (Ehsanifar & Rubin, 2011). Internal customer are employees in the next stage process. External customers are end customers of the process. This seems contrary to the view that lean must satisfy external customers. Moreover, in the past, the company has focused on customer, the internal customers. External customers must respond and if they fail to respond, the product is modified, the prices are adjusted, or a new marketing strategy is conducted (Salman, 2017). However, if you remember that external customers are the end customers, then the internal customers actually respond to external ones. What is valuable to external customers, therefore, is also valuable to internal customers. Absolutely, the main destination is on the end customers as external, not the customers in the internal.

Prioritizing customers is not lean monopoly. Various methods of improving quality lead to customers. Similarly, many companies place the word "customer" in the company's vision and mission. However, lean does not only have it as a slogan or artifact. Focus on customer is conducted by lean and is a part of the corporate culture. It has become the employee's basic values, beliefs, and assumptions (Liker & Morgan, 2006).

Value is determined by customers themselves. This is important, so the process steps fully contain the values that customers care about. It is the nature of process to grow and become more complex over time. Without holding on to customers, this growing process will increase costs and perhaps some of these costs are not needed because it does not increase value for customer. The point is, lean process is a process with minimal waste and maximum value for customers.

A good approach to know the customer value is by asking the questions: what customers want and what they are willing to pay. The goods that make customer want and willing to pay are values. The goods that customers do not want and do not want to pay for are waste or *muda*. There are seven types of waste (Julien, 2011):

1. Overproduction: The company produces too many goods. Customers will not buy goods beyond their needs. Even if there is a desire that is exceeding the need, perhaps because of an attractive promotion or a powerful marketing strategy, the amount of purchased goods will remain limited. Moreover, these goods are bought because of the discount price, which, in turn, decreases profits per unit or because the goods are only to be consumed before new goods are restocked.
2. Waiting time: Companies use time ineffectively. Consequently, customer have to queue or wait for goods to arrive. The longer the queue or waiting time, the lower the customer desire to buy at the price. They will demand compensation and therefore prices will be lower. They will even switch to faster providers without queues.
3. Transportation: Waste of transportation is related to the movement of product components between processes without adding value. This results in various problems such as queues, failures, etc., that are not considered valuable by customers.

4. Inappropriate processing: For example, due to the use of central process on several lines queue and delay will occur. The output can also be late and does not meet customer's expectation.
5. Unnecessary reserves: Reserve encourages companies to spend it to avoid decaying of reserves before processing. The result will be the same as wasting excessive production.
6. Unnecessary movement: movements such as movement among chutes or walking between procedures will waste energy and costs. Customers do not want to pay for this, so the profits will decrease.
7. Failed product: The customers will not buy failed products. Even if they want to buy, they will buy them in very cheap price, even cheaper than the production costs. The company sells it only to keep it from losing too much.

Based on waste, a process in manufacturing products is divided into three types (Julien, 2011):

1. Adding-value activities according to customers
2. Non-direct adding-value activities, but required to deliver value to customers
3. Any non-adding value activities appreciated by customers

Meanwhile, when viewed from the position in process, there are three types of activities (Julien, 2011):

1. Problem-solving: It is the activity starting from product concept, design, engineering, testing, production, and launching.
2. Information management: This is a process of taking orders, scheduling, and shipping.
3. Physical transformation: This activity is real product manufacturing.

Usually, the main customers are used as references. The company with the main customer representatives will conduct an analysis of their needs. The company will challenge its customers' old view value with a new one since it is possible that what is considered valuable in the past is worthless in the present.

Prioritizing customers will help in solving internal conflicts in product design. Liker and Morgan (2006) provide examples of conflicts between stylists and engineers in automotive product design. Often, these two works go into conflict. The problem is, stylists prioritize beauty and appearance because they are artists. However, this beauty and appearance can only be beautiful or elegant from a stylist's perspective. Moreover, beauty and good appearance can sacrifice valuable aspects from engineers' perspective. Engineers prioritize the value of functionality and manufacturability. They might produce poor designs from artist's perspective, but they have high functionality and manufacturability. If the two parties are met, not necessarily both of them see a conflict. Therefore, the voice of customers must be heard. It could be that customers choose fine art cars or cars with dual functionality, or in-between, or others. Stylists and engineers are no longer prioritizing their interests but what the customers expect.

Another example is problem of arranging items by the chef. A chef can arrange a fork box on the left and a spoon box on the right. The reason might be simply because the fork starts from the letter F, while the spoon from the letter S. The chef might view alphabetical value as valuable to them. However, do the customers care or not care about the fork and spoon box order?

As the first step to lean, determining customer value can touch the aspects of organizational beliefs. The production or distribution configuration may change, and so do the product cost and diversity. Companies often think that to increase profits, they will make a variety of products whether various flavors, various shapes, and so on. However, it could be that some of these variants are actually waste because they are not desired by customers. It could be that existing products must have additional costs to meet customer's desire. Delivery can become a little longer because customers do not want it now. Indeed, it seems this is contrary to the efforts to reduce costs or time, but it is actually efficient when it is viewed from a wider perspective. Note that cost reduction and time reduction are based on the customer's point of view, not the company's point of view. A waste adds time and cost but does not add value. The aspects that add value, even though they add time and costs, are not a waste. The point is, the focus is on adding value to customers and reducing non-adding-value aspects.

The formulated customer values need to be rethought in a certain time periodically. This ensures the cycle of lean principles runs well. The process can run fast in one day. However, in a certain time according to various considerations, customer values need to be re-examined.

Furthermore, customer values must be identified as accurately as possible. Accuracy is necessary to obtain the right vision on target, included the costs needed to meet these customer values. This cost needs to be a basis for eliminating waste. The target cost is incurred cost in a situation where there is no waste at all. This cost is always lower than that of the competitors. Therefore, in this way, companies can make future direction for their products.

Toyota has a system called *Obeya*. This system adjusts, implements, tracks, and provides customer-based goals for the working team (Liker and Morgan, 2006). *Obeya* means "big room". In this system, the chief engineer and functional managers hold meetings in a large room at least every few days. Sometimes, the meetings are held every day. In this meeting, the focus is on the integration of all car parts. Participants use visual management to show graphs of trends, schedules, problems, and problem-solving, as well as other information that describe the projects' status in all functional groups. *Obeya* can improve communication and decision-making between chief engineers and functional managers.

However, because it focuses on customer value, lean will add value, create value, and eliminate non-value aspects. Adding value means increasing the existing product's value. The product already has the desired value by customers, but the accuracy of given value by the previous product is not quite good. In added-value products, the given value is more accurate according to the customer's expectation. Creating value means bring out new values from the product. The previous product does not contain this value. Based on the customer's evaluation, companies feel the products must have that value and therefore create value for customers.

Shamah (2013) mentions the core activities of value creation including the following:

1. Increasing product benefits and uses through better quality, function, or image
2. Reducing costs through production, efficiency, and other ways to change attitudes and thoughts

Furthermore, these two value creation activities need to meet the below requirements (Shamah, 2013):

1. Distantly related, meaning it converts input into output that can be sold.
2. Mediated, meaning connecting customers in a network. The customers and customer network lead to the company which provides services to the network.

3. Intensive, meaning problem-solving is conducted by the experts and applying expertise. Experts do not have to be academic. They can be employees who are responsible for certain production processes who understand how the process works.

Meanwhile, according to Salman (2017), the process of adding value contains some conditions including the following:

1. Changes of information or material or reduce uncertainty
2. Customers are willing to pay for it
3. Conducted right from the start

To further understand the concept of value, let us have a look at an example of health service training. Health service training has seven types of customers: community, training institution, insurance, government, entrepreneurs, students, and faculty/staff. Each of these customer groups has its own value for health service training. Values for each customer group are as follows (Bame, 2017):

1. Community
   a. Quality health services
   b. Affordable health services
   c. Access on health services
2. Training institutions
   a. Continuous and steady student flow
   b. Expectation to obtain medical knowledge
   d. Achieve certain tasks related to patients: clinical training
3. Insurance
   a. Affordable cost services
   b. Customers do not have to use an insurance/health service system: preventive services
   c. Low error rate (high service quality): re-working
4. Government
   a. Health service access to all citizens
   b. Reduction of unemployment
   c. Service quality
5. Entrepreneurs
   a. Having well-trained and ready-to-work employees
   b. Students' availability to work when needed

6. Students
   a. Adequate education/certification to pursue a career/job
   b. Obtain job after graduation
   c. Affordable tuition fee
7. Faculty/staff
   a. Permanent fulltime job
   b. Promotion/compensation for achievements

Chapter 12

What is Stream?

From a customer's perspective, there are some activities or steps in company that are ignored. Meaning, it does not flow in customer value stream but in company value. If the company prioritizes and optimizes its value, then customer value stream is likely to be marginalized and therefore customers are ignored (Bozdogan et al., 2000). Therefore, it is very important for companies to visualize and balance the stream of flowing values throughout the main stakeholders (Bozdogan et al., 2000:39).

The step after determining the value is to identify the value stream. To maintain clarity, in the next discussion, we call it as value stream, while the stream is referred as stream. This value stream identification is actually a very technical process and we will give it in detail in the next book. We will go straight to the next step in lean principle, which is to make the stream running smoothly for the value stream.

In simple terms, the efforts to smoothly run the stream value are only by removing all types of inhibitors, defilements, and backflow from existing processes (Ehsanifar & Rubin, 2011:29). The ideal stream for lean is the continuous stream of products along the value stream from raw materials to end customers.

While waste is the focus of value stream principles, variability is the focus of stream principle. Variability is any deviation in services or products that creates unnecessary costs (Bhatia & Drew, 2007). Lean goals can even be seen as an effort to reduce stream variability. This step prevents interference with the process during its implementation (Norberg, 2008).

Variability results in a process stream flowing slowly. Process stream may not slow down because of process design. Customers must be able to move throughout the process and not get caught. This can be illustrated as a ship that is sailing in a river. If there is a sharp narrow stream, for instance, due to a turn that reaches almost 360 degrees, the ship can get caught. Smoothing of stream functions to make the river removes the sharp turns. In a smooth stream, the boat can easily sail from its starting point to its final point.

Another example of stream smoothing comes from Norberg (2008). Norberg gave an example of traffic on a highway. If only all vehicles on the highway run at the same speed, the distance between vehicles can be made very small without any accident at all. However, because the speed is almost same and each vehicle depends on the vehicle in front of it, there is no variation in the gap between the vehicles. However, in reality, a vehicle makes a gap from other vehicles to avoid accidents. Moreover, the gap will also change because the speed is different. In rush hour situations, the gap between the vehicles will shorten. In this situation, one vehicle speed variation will affect other vehicles, increasing the accident risk. As a result, speed variation must be immediately responded by other vehicles.

There are three steps to create stream in the process. All three steps must be conducted entirely (Ehsanifar & Rubin, 2011):

1. Focus on the entire product from the beginning to the end. This step will provide a holistic picture of entire supply chain.
2. Ignore the traditional boundaries of work, career, function, and company. This is different between traditional organizations and lean organizations. Traditional organizations specialize in each department in a specific field, have large batches in the system, produce products based on predictions, accumulate inventory, and are centered on costs. Meanwhile, lean organizations are process oriented by replacing batch processing with one-piece flow, minimizing inventory, and focusing on customer's actual value.
3. Rethink specific work practices and tools to remove backflow, obstruction, or defilement of all types in the stream, for instance, the additional design process waste. It is possible to conduct the same two steps in value stream but they are conducted in different times. This results in additional resources and increases total waiting time in the process.

Improvement of stream is a sustainable step. Experimenting new solutions and improving the process stream will lead to new conditions which in turn

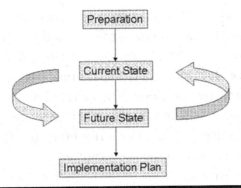

Figure 12.1   Cycle of process stream (Kim et al., 2006).

lead to new future condition (Kim, Spahlinger, Kin, & Billi, 2006). These steps occur because smoothing the process stream cannot be perfect in only one cycle. Even if perfect, there will be disruptions, obstacles, and new backflows that sometimes require new solutions currently as well as in the future. This cyclical situation is indicated in Figure 12.1.

Variability in stream is known as *mura*. *Mura* is a non-similar production speed. In the car industry in Japan, this problem is sometimes resolved by *takotei-mochi*. *Takotei-mochi* is providing multi-task work throughout the process stream (Teece & Pisano, 2004).

The main reason for unsteady stream is due to a bottleneck. Bottleneck occurs if the requirements that come into one phase have a higher level than that of submitted to the next phase. Bottleneck removal will increase the smooth flow and overall output of the process. This is addressed by bottleneck detection. Bottleneck detection is conducted by (1) identifying obstacles, (2) identifying causes of obstacles, (3) removing obstacles, and (4) returning to Step 1 (Petersen & Wohlin, 2009).

Generally, waste that often occurs in the process stream is waste of transportation, wasteful processes, and product defects (Robinson, Radnor, Burgess, & Worthington, 2012):

1. Transportation waste arises due to unnecessary movement of products to conduct the process. This waste is detected by the transportation time in a slowing process stream. If there is a slowdown, there may be a product that makes unnecessary movements.
2. Process waste occurs due to poor product design tools or activities. This waste is detected by the use of resources and processes in excessive process stream. If there is a waste of resources and processes, the process stream will not run smoothly.

3. Defective products result in efforts to examine and correct the defect. Defective product and its impact are detected in the process stream through interconnection in the process stream. If a product is suddenly interconnected or disappeared from the process stream, it is a sign that the product is defective or poor. The officer has to remove it from the process stream, so it will not interfere the next step. Absolutely, it is better if this defective product does not enter the process stream. Waste exists in the process stream to the point where the product is removed from the process stream.

Besides waste (*muda*), of course, *mura* and *muri* can be observed from the process stream. *Mura* is observed as a result of variability in stream speed, whereas *muri* is observed from the use of resources, including workers and staff, excess and bottleneck in stream (Robinson et al., 2012).

There are four types of process streams in a company (Ehsanifar and Rubin, 2011):

1. Design process stream: the stream in creating a product prototype.
2. Order-taking process stream: the stream in taking orders or specification from customers.
3. Production process stream: the stream to change the raw material into the final product.
4. Distribution process stream: the stream from taking the final product to the external customers.

However, because the formation of process stream is not simple and easy, an ideal starting point is needed where flow can be as simple and easy as possible. According to Ehsanifar and Rubin (2011), a good starting point to begin the process stream is the final product of production process stream. This final product is called a pacemaker. From here, the stream can run smoothly to the upstream.

Lean tools that can be used to create smooth stream include (Ehsanifar and Rubin, 2011)

1. Transparency and visual control: Visual control allows the process to be visualized and facilitates direct and thorough observation to the process. This visual control is an example of a value stream mapping (VSM). VSM provides an overview of value stream in all processes

involved in creating a product or service and also describes critical process metrics such as cycle time, touch time, and queue time (Parnell-Klabo, 2006).

2. Standardization and 5S: Standardization ensures that variability is easily detected. 5S develops the activity of sorting and straightening the working environment to facilitate detection of waste and irregularities.

3. Status indicator: As the name implies, it signifies the status of steps in the process, so it can be easily observed whether the process is running as it should or it has a problem.

involved in creating a product or service and also describe grid
cal process metrics such as cycle time, total time, and queue time
(Carnell-Kimbo, 2000).

2. Standardization of 5S: Standardization ensures that variability is easily
detected. 5S develops the activity of sorting and simplifies the the work
the environment to facilitate detection of waste and irregularities.

3. Status indicator: As the name implies, it signifies the status of steps in
the process so it can be easily observed whether the process is running
as it should or it has a problem.

Chapter 13

Pull Concept

We arrive at the most misunderstood principle in lean, the pull concept. Pull basically responds to customer's attraction or customer's needs. It involves the process designs that are able to respond on customer's demand changes. It is often called as JIT or "Just in Time".

The misunderstanding in pull concept is that it is interpreted as making a product when the customers demand it. This is a tactical concept of pull. There are two types of pull concepts, the first is strategic pull and second is tactical pull. Strategic pull merely limits the amount of work in the process in the system. Tactical pull, as already mentioned, manufactures the product only after the order is made. The concept of tactical pull is not always right. For instance, it is impossible for a seller in a store to supply goods when ordered by customers. Customers obviously want to visit the store, pick up goods, then leave, not waiting for the item to be ordered by the store. Meanwhile, the concept of strategic pull is always right. Companies must always limit the amount of work in process optimally in the sense that they have almost no inventory. In other words, existing inventory have anticipated customer needs in the real terms. Therefore, we must understand the pull concept as a strategic pull concept.

According to Hopp and Spearman (2004), there are three reasons why pull system can improve system performance:

1. Less congestion: Congestion occurs because of bottleneck in process stream and due to the large amount of work in the previous process but the next process cannot handle it.

2. Easier control: Work in process is easier to control than product output because:
   a. Work in process is easier to be observed directly than product output.
   b. Product output is controlled based on capacity. This capacity is estimated through process time, setup time, random outages, worker efficiency, rework, and other factors. Work in process can be directly observed immediately.
   c. Output is controlled by determining input level. If the capacity of the line is greater than input rate, output level will be equal to the input level. If not, the output is equal to capacity and there will be accumulation in the stream. If the capacity is incorrectly calculated, stream error can occur. However, if the work in process is controlled, the system will flow easily.
3. Work in process cap: It makes the stream run smoothly according to its stream capacity.

The pull concept is strategically based on standard work methods (autonomy) and level scheduling. Meanwhile, pull system is tactically dealing with maintaining the production rate equal to the takt time and adjusting it continuously (Ehsanifar & Rubin, 2011). Takt time is production rate. It is set according to customer's demand level. It is called by takt time as each order requires time to be implemented. Takt time is given by

$$T = H/W$$

where T is the takt time, H is the number of available hours in one work period, and W is the number of working units need to be completed in one day (Lempia, 2008).

If there is an error in process, the time in pull system can be sacrificed because the product is in minimal production. For this reason, a number of inspection activities were conducted as follows (Biswas, 2013):

1. Independent inspection
   a. Inspection by the operator on the product when it is manufactured
   b. Inspection by downstream operator when they receive the product
   c. Fool proofing (*poka yoke*) and standardization
   d. Supplier process control

2. Inspection provides a number of procedures that must be maintained by the operator (Biswas, 2013):
   a. Never allow a defective/poor product to be pull in your work station.
   b. Never make a defective/poor product in your work station.
   c. Never allow a defective/poor part pull from your work station.

According to Jansson et al. (2009), pull principle implementation in lean process includes a number of procedures:

a. Keep the production system flexible on customer's demand.
b. Make the production system adapt to customer's demand in the future.
c. Be aware to reduce waiting time and cycle time.
d. Work until the last moment under the company responsibility.

Meanwhile, Hopp and Spearman (2004) recommend a number of steps to guarantee the pull process, namely:

a. Eliminate obvious waste: overcome the easy problems first and then the more difficult ones. Identification is performed by value stream map and 5S.
b. Increase inventory buffer to isolate problems in fabrication.
c. Reduce variability in the substream and final stream.
d. Reduce inventory buffer after problem is resolved.
e. Address other more difficult problems in fabrication.

In industrial practice, there are several types of pull system implementations (Hopp and Spearman, 2004):

1. *Kanban:* *Kanban* is a line production system using cards as a signal to continue production or other process. The number of *kanban* cards determines the limit on number of works in process.
2. Constant work in process (CONWIP): The CONWIP system is a modified *kanban* system. In CONWIP, first station in the stream performs a pull signal (*kanban* card) but the other station does not perform it. Therefore, all operators except the first station behave the same as they are in a push system by processing work when they obtain it. The cards in CONWIP function as line specific, while in *kanban*, it functions as product parts specific.

3. *K, S* system (Liberopoulos & Dallery, 2002): *K* is the limit of work in process, whereas *S* is the basic stock. A system is classified as pull system if $K < \infty$ or, in other words, work in process is limited. *K* is determined by manufacture facilities, whereas *S* is determined by product store.

4. POLKA system: Similar to *kanban* and CONWIP, this system limits work in process.

5. PAC system: Classified as pull system if the number of process tags is less than infinite. Process tag functions to limit number of works in process.

6. Material requirement planning (MRP) with work-in-process obstacles. MRP without work-in-process obstacles is a push system but if it is controlled by work in process it becomes a pull system.

The example of methods above distinguish between pull system and push system. According to Hopp and Spearman (2004), a strategic push system is a system that does not provide a real limit on the amount of work in process that may exist in the system. Systems classified as a push system are as follows (Hopp and Spearman, 2004):

1. MRP: MRP is a push system because products are made according to the main production schedule regardless of system status. There is no limit on work in process.

2. Classic base stock system: There is no limit on work in process on this system. This is because backorders can increase beyond the base stock level.

3. Installation stock (*Q, r*): (*Q, r*) is an echelon stock. There is no limit on order numbers in this system.

4. *K, S* system: *K* is the work in process limit, whereas *S* is the base stock. *K* is determined by manufacture facilities, whereas *S* is determined by product store. If *K* is infinite, then the system is a push system.

5. PAC system: It is classified as a push system if number of process tags is infinite.

Hopp and Spearman (2004) state that a product that is produced based on predictions does not have to be a push system and likewise, products made on order do not have to be a pull system. Table 13.1 indicates when the pull and push systems are applied on three types of product manufacturing bases.

Table 13.1 Pull and Push System Based on Product Manufacturing

	Make-to-Forecast	*Make-to-Order*	*Make-to-Stock*
Push	MRP with forecast	MRP with company order	(Q, r) with pull from finished goods inventory (FGI)
Pull	*Kanban* with takt time and forecast	*Kanban* with takt time and order	*Kanban* with pull from FGI

Source: Hopp and Spearman (2004).

Table 13.2 Tactical Differences of Pull System and Push System

	Pull System	*Push System*
Production signal	From downstream processes – based on actual customer's demand	From upstream processes – based on scheduled/predicted demand
Pros	Can accommodate uncertain customer demand; very responsive to customers	Most flexible on product diversity; not susceptible to long waiting time
Cons	Not suitable for end product diversity	Not responsive to customers unless the waiting time is very fast
Needs of waiting time	Requires fast waiting time to react on uncertain customer demand	Less susceptible to waiting time because they are formed according to schedule
Fast waiting time	Reducing inventory, not reducing responsiveness on customers	Encourage responsiveness on customers
Product diversity	Low end-product diversity	High end-product diversity
Inventory location	Most inventory is in the final goods	Most inventories are in raw materials

Source: Vessell (2006:19).

Table 13.2 indicates the tactical difference between pull and push systems according to Vessel (2006).

Vessel illustrates the difference of pull system in Figure 13.1. From this figure, it can be observed that pull system (Quick Burger Production Line) starts from customer orders which then leads to the employees taking raw materials from the refrigerator. The worker then cooks, assembles, and provides it on the Warming Table. Warming Table serves to store the final

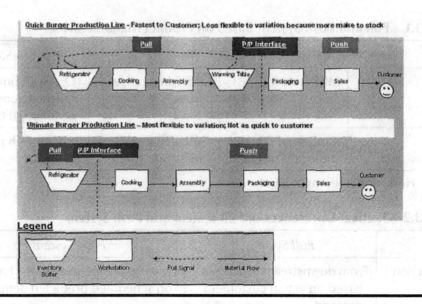

Figure 13.1   Illustration of pull and push system differences (Vessell, 2006).

product before delivering to the customers by the receptionist who serves orders from the next customers. From Warming Table, the products are packaged and sold to customers directly by a push system. Meanwhile, in Ultimate Burger, customer orders are responded by pulling raw materials from the refrigerator, then cooked, assembled, packaged, and finally sold to the customers.

In pull system, there is a buildup of final product in Warming Table, while in push system, there is a buildup of raw materials in the refrigerator. However, because buildup is in the form of raw materials, push system responds easily on variations in customer's demands. Meanwhile, pull system is less in responding to variations, since the final products are already on Warming Table and for new types of products, it needs a processing time from refrigerator to the Warming Table. However, pull system responds more quickly to customers because the final products are available in Warming Table. Meanwhile, push system has to face difficulties to provide fast service because everything starts from the earliest point.

Chapter 14

Pull Impact

In the previous chapter, we have observed the advantages and disadvantages of applying tactical pull system in a process stream. Papadopoulou (2013) specifically examines the impact of pull system on job-store performance. He found that control mechanism of pure pull system using *kanban* has superior performance in the majority of criteria compared with push system. Table 14.1 indicates the performance of pull and push systems in non-repetitive manufacturing system in a multinational company.

Table 14.1 shows that almost all performance indicators indicate the superiority of pure pull system compared with two types of modified pull systems (*kanban* and constant work in process (CONWIP)) as well as base stock push system. There is only one low indicator that is the average engine usage. Pure pull system uses machine at an average of 3% higher rate than other systems.

Tommelein (1998) used simulation to compare pull model with two variations of push model in pipe installation project. Two variations of push model represented two extreme points in the coordination. The first model was a completely chaotic model where there was no coordination among the fabrication part and the installation part in running the project at all. As a result, what was produced by division of fabrication might be different to what was needed by installation division. The second model was a perfect coordinated model where all team members ideally coordinated. What the factory made was always the same as what was needed by the installation team. The third model was pull model where division of factory produced materials that did not necessarily match the installation requirements. Even so, the installation division on the first shipment provided feedback about

Table 14.1 Performance of Pull System versus Push System

Performance Metrics	Pure Pull System	Kanban	Base Stock	CONWIP
Total output time (hour)	1,148	4,192	2,789	12,502
Average stream time (hour)	25	102	74	269
Producing time (hour)	175	293	253	492
Earliness (hour)	184	0	0	0
Lateness (hour)	485	4,192	2,789	12,502
Lateness – Earliness (hour)	301	4,192	2,789	12,502
Number of late works	21	50	50	50
Filling rate (%)	0	0	0	0
Machine average idle (%)	3	1	2	1
Work in process level (works)	7	27	32	31
Total queuing time (hour)	755	6,909	7,417	13,648
Total setup time (hour)	351	1,104	922	1,690

Source: Papadopoulou (2013).

its requirements in the fabrication division. As a result, the activities were always been updated, so that the needed products by the installation division were prioritized by the factory.

The results of simulation are indicated in Figure 14.1. It can be seen that the random model takes 400 days to complete the project. The number of accumulated product parts in the location is very huge because it has not been used or it is not used. On the 250th day, the number of goods piled up to a maximum of 500.

The perfect model was able to complete the project on 250th day, and the number of items piled up was much lower at only 200. The largest pile up was on the 100th day. The pull model has a completion period of 300 days. The amount of goods piled up around 250 at the maximum point, on the 125th day.

Figure 14.1 actually indicates that pull model performs lower than the perfect coordination model. However, Tommelein (1998) asserts that the pull model is very suitable to be used in construction projects. This is because the perfect coordination model is an ideal model. This model cannot be actualized in the real world because there is no way for a project to run perfectly. Installation projects are conducted in the field that always changes

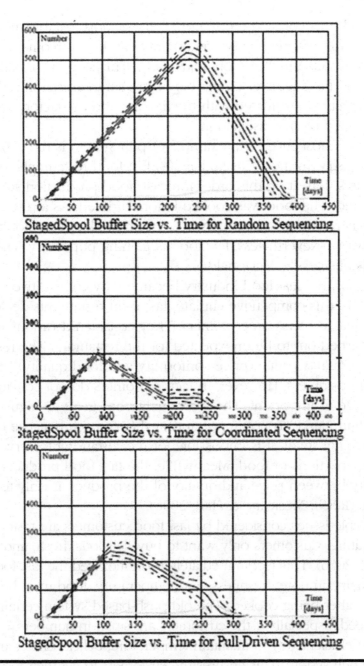

Figure 14.1 **Random, perfect, and pull models (Tommelein, 1998).**

its specific conditions. Each installation location will have different specifications and hence will not be in line with the regular fabrication situation. Further, there are not only factories and installers in the field. There are many stakeholders involved and each of them may have their own specifications of what the factory expects.

In line with this condition, pull model is the most suitable model with the reality that is full of uncertainty. Uncertainty can be overcome by feedback (pull) which results in fabrication adjustment. This step ensures that progress is efficient and flexible. Every time there is a change in specifications, this change is directly coordinated with the factory, and the factory produces the products needed by the installation.

Perhaps the most successful example of pull system is the evolution of fast food industry. In the 1970s and 1980s, fast food restaurants used predictable orders. Based on this order forecast, food production schedule was conducted. The food was cooked before ordered. As a result, waste was everywhere. Many foods that were not ordered and cannot be stored, became a waste. Nevertheless, fast food is gaining popularity. The main actor in this business is McDonald.

In the 1980s, the fast food industry became very competitive (Taylor & Lyon, 1995). In this competitive climate, fast food restaurants decided to focus on valuable issues on customers. They considered various factors. The result turned out to be unexpected for the restaurant. The restaurants believed that quality, value (price conformity and food quality), and size are valuable for customers. However, in fact, customers do not consider quality, value, and size as important. The food quality has great ambiguity. Food size (small, medium, large) is not important for the stomach because the variations are actually small. It is impossible for the restaurant to serve very little or very large portions of food. Meanwhile, the fast food products' value, the compatibility between price and quality of the product, is only temporary and relative (Reich, Mccleary, & Hall, 2006).

The valuable issues considered by fast food customers are taste, freshness, and temperature. Customers only want to buy delicious, fresh, and warm food (Reich et al., 2006). This fact immediately revolutionized the fast food business world. To maintain taste, freshness, and temperature, food must be consumed immediately after being cooked. The old push-based system certainly cannot meet this need, especially if the customers are small in numbers.

The most efficient way to maintain temperature, deliciousness, and freshness is using the pull system. This ensures the customers to get their food as soon as they order at the right temperature and fresh condition. Work standardization guarantees that products have consistent taste. Furthermore, they also use fresh products by getting their supplies directly from raw material companies or farmers. A slogan then appeared "we don't make it until you order it".

The first adopter of pull system in fast food industry is Burger King as they try to defeat McDonald (Taylor and Lyon, 1995). Since the 1990s until now, pull system in the fast food industry has become popular. The demand starts from the cash register where the order is made. The cashier then sends an electronic signal to the kitchen and the production begins. Kitchen design must be made as efficient as possible to allow motion, or in other words, no waste of motion. This flexible cell design allows all materials to be stored in the right order. After cooking, workers arrange each item based on the standardized work procedures. Production flows according to the standard rhythms. The production ends when the product is on the customers' tray and the satisfaction is determined by how quickly the food reaches the customer (Lian, 2006).

Particular fast food companies such as McDonald even makes drive-through services. Besides relying on speed, this system relies on the layout efficiency. Pull system forces fast food customers who use drive-through service to move around the building, rather than stop at one point and deliver the order like regular customers. Drive-through customers do not mind this system because they move using vehicles. Orders are made at the starting point. This order is automatic without being served by a waiter. Of course, there is a waiter at the end of the microphone who records the orders from customers. This order is then made as the customers move to cashier. At the cash register, customers pay for the ordered product while the food is still in process. Food is sent to the food delivery window as the customers move to the window. The drive-through system layout is indicated in Figure 14.2.

From Figure 14.2, we can see the position of order point, the payment window, and the product delivery window. Behind this window, there is raw material storage which is cyclic and clockwise, according to the process flow. From the storage, the process goes to the sandwich fries, and finally packaging area (right side of payment window). From packaging, the product is sent to the drive-through customers on the right side through delivery window, or delivered to the cashier for customers in the counter.

The speed and flexibility in producing the products is an advantage for fast food companies. This is more beneficial considering that almost no food is wasted.

However, keep in mind that taste, as the main value of fast food customers, is a significantly varying value. Various kinds of flavors and constantly consuming food with the same taste is boring. Based on this fact, many fast food companies are improving their product variety. However, the increase in product variation sacrifices the service speed. The more the variety of products, the greater the waiting time. The production speed of one product is different from other products. One order with three variations will

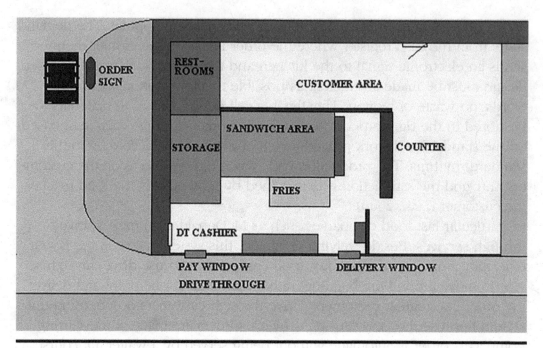

Figure 14.2 Drive-through system (Whiting & Weckman, 2004).

be delivered at the longest product time. Let us say a customer orders three products, one with a waiting time of 5 minutes, one with a waiting time of 10 minutes, and the other with a waiting time of 4 minutes. In this case, the customer will receive full order after 10 minutes.

In the beginning, fast food restaurants competed to produce a variety of products. McDonald, for instance, once had more than 150 types of products, which were later reduced to be only 33 (Taylor and Lyon, 1995). After becoming aware of the time that they scarified, they began to limit their products to various strategies so that the waiting time was not too long. They may release new food regularly while hiding the old food from the poster or completely remove it from the menu, especially the least salable food or food with the longest waiting time. Another strategy is creating variations on minor details such as sauces, cooking methods, and so on. This small variation makes it seem like a big difference.

As a result of these two different directions, focus on speed and on variation, two types of fast food restaurants emerge: restaurants with little menus but fast service, and restaurants with many menus but slow service. Including in the category of fast service restaurants is Kentucky Fried Chicken (KFC), whereas restaurants with many menu services is Pizza Hut. However, they have their own degree of speed and variety. KFC, although fast, still tries to present new products regularly while removing non-selling-well products. Similarly, Pizza Hut has standardized on their pizza templates, although the ingredients of pizza can vary.

Another example of pull system benefit is given by Adnan, Jaffar, Yusoff, and Halim (2013). Adnan et al.'s research was conducted on *kanban* system as a solution to uncertainty due to fluctuations in customer's demand and requirements. They conducted research on Proton automotive parts company in Malaysia. They designed a pull system with the following stages:

1. Withdraw *kanban* PW card from Heijunka post according to pitch time
2. Take empty polyboxes based on PWK card quantity
3. Supply empty polyboxes
4. Exchange PI with PW and put FG onto trolley
5. Make lots; save PI in the lot form post when PI number meets the specific quantity and place it into *kanban* chute
6. Move the finished goods to gate-Q or warehouse line
7. Repeat task number 1

These steps are illustrated in Figure 14.3.

Pull system implementation on Proton automotive parts company results in 5% decrease in waiting time from the previous 10.7 days to 6.9 days; reduce the number of inventory in the process from 4,840 to only 2,321 (a decrease of 52%); reduce the area of finished goods by 4%, and reduce 55% of finished goods from 1,780 pieces to only 794 pieces (Adnan et al., 2013).

Roh, Hong, and Min (2014) tested statistically the effect of pull system on organization responsiveness in the market. Pull production is defined as a degree to which a particular action program, related to batch reduction, setup time reduction, and use of *kanban* system, is conducted. Meanwhile, organization responsiveness to the market is a report on operational performance in terms of time to market, speed of delivery, dependence on shipping, and manufacturing waiting time. The reason is because the product is made only when the customer requests it, then the responsiveness to the market will certainly increase. If there is a production change or an upstream problem, the downstream process will be closed, thus preventing inventory buildup on the downstream. Fluctuation reduction in the inventory level of work in process shortens cycle times and increases responsiveness to market demand. Moreover, pull system supports mass customization which is a determinant of market responsiveness. The results of analysis on 559 manufacturing units from 24 countries in the world by Roh et al. (2014) have proved that pull production significantly increases organization responsiveness to the market. The

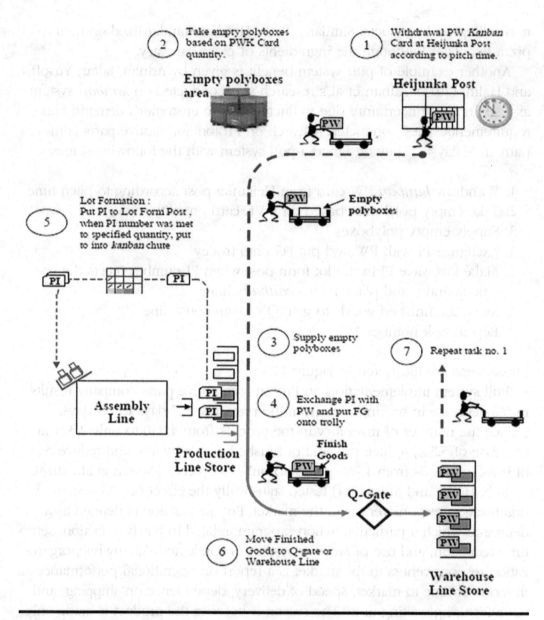

Figure 14.3 *Kanban* procedures on proton parts (Adnan et al., 2013).

more frequent the company plans its business and takes action to implement pull production, the higher the company market operational performance.

Roh et al. (2014) also provided clues to the factors that affect pull production. This study found that pull production was positively affected by two issues, namely, collaboration with suppliers and advanced manufacturing technology. Collaboration with suppliers is the expansion of coordinated planned decisions and goods flow and physical interaction with the key and strategic suppliers. This is indicated by a demand that suppliers managed or hold inventories in the factories owned by the company, planning, forecasting, and collaborative refilling, and physical integration of suppliers with factories. The higher the collaboration with suppliers, the higher pull process occurring in the supplied companies. In other words, collaboration with suppliers is one of the success factors for implementing pull system in the company. This makes sense because the supplier is needed to reduce inventory level so that the pull production system can run well. Good partnership with suppliers allows the suppliers to help companies increase their manufacturing flexibility and hence successfully use the lean manufacturing tools and techniques needed for pull production by reducing cycle times. However, because pull system increases responsiveness to market changes, collaboration with strategic suppliers will in turn increase the company responsiveness on market changes.

Advanced manufacturing technology is the expansion of operational activities using automatic technology for loading and unloading tasks, vehicle guidance, and inventory retrieval system. Advanced manufacturing technology is also a key factor for the success of pull process. This process occurs because advanced manufacturing technology allows manufacturing flexibility and reduces replacement time and consequently supports time-based manufacturing practices. The example of companies that have suc-cessfully used advanced technology to support their pull system are Toyota and LG Mobile.

Interestingly, Roh et al.'s (2014) study did not find that pull process was affected by sharing knowledge with customers. Sharing knowledge with customers is the use of electronic devices with key and strategic customers to access vital information, collaboration, and service preparation. This includes data analysis (audit and reporting), access to catalog, order management and tracking, content and knowledge management, and collaborative support services. Initially, Roh et al. (2014) considered that this relationship exists. This is due to the opinion that a flexible production schedule is a prerequisite for pull production system, and a flexible production schedule is supplied by easy access to customer demand information. External customers can send demand which is then responded by the company. In fact, it is the customer's demand that triggers pull system. Likewise, internal customers such as employees can immediately address potential production problems based on informa-tion obtained from these customers, so the flow of materials is undisturbed. A popular example is Boeing which replaces the batch system configuration and long queue with the principle of manufacturing a single piece based on real-time demand information. The practice of sharing information should be

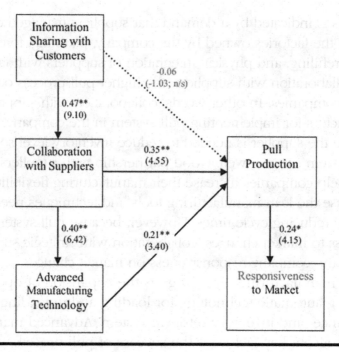

Figure 14.4   Pull system determinants (Roh et al., 2014).

a factor for pull production system because uninterrupted material flow and flexible production are very important for pull system implementation.

The finding that sharing knowledge with customers does not have an impact on pull system actually occurs directly. Indirectly, knowledge sharing with customers has an effect on pull production through collaboration with suppliers. Meaning that, only if customer's demand is responded through cooperation with suppliers, the pull system can work. If there is no collaboration with suppliers, the demand addressed by customers on company does not bring an increase in pull system. This is due to the demand system that must be sent to the company's upstream partners as a part of feedback in pull system. The company's capability to share and send information to the supplier is very important because the supplier is important in keeping the system with a minimum inventory. Figure 14.4 indicates the relationship among affecting and affected variables by pull system in the company.

Note that in Figure 14.4, collaboration with suppliers also has a positive effect on the use of manufacturing technology which drives the pull production. This is due to the strong relationship between company's organizational flexibility related to collaboration with the advanced manufacturing technology. Companies are more likely to explore advanced manufacturing technology than companies without partnership with suppliers and customers.

Chapter 15

How to Pursue Perfection

Improvement is complete waste elimination in a system. Improvement brings new opportunities to eliminate waste and provide value. The idea is to continually refine the process and continue to work on lean principles cycle.

Improvement consists of two complementary approaches, namely, *kaikaku* and *kaizen* (Ehsanifar & Rubin, 2011). The difference lies in the nature of improvement. *Kaizen* is an improvement with small steps, process-and-HR-oriented and sustainable, whereas *kaikaku* is an episodic improvement, fundamental, aims to achieve dramatic results, and a top-down initiative (Yamamoto, 2010). The point is *kaikaku* as a revolutionary change, whereas *kaizen* is evolutionary change. This difference can be seen in Figure 15.1.

It can be seen that *kaikaku* is a short-term change with a sudden increase in performance, whereas *kaizen* is a change in a slower and more sustainable time with a production performance that does not change sharply.

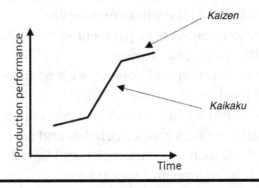

Figure 15.1   Differences of *kaizen* and *kaikaku* (Yamamoto, 2010).

Kaikaku

Kaikaku makes radical and fundamental changes needed by the company to be a lean company (Ehsanifar and Rubin, 2011). This radical change is an improvement beginning with rethinking of the existing processes (Arnheiter & Maleyeff, 2005). *Kaikaku* aims to find new radical models in a completely new sense. Sometimes, radical changes are needed to completely change the wasteful situation (Scherger, 2005). Yamamoto (2010) identified the existence of four *kaikaku* based on two dimensions, namely, innovation and implementation:

1. Innovation includes radical and incremental innovations.
   a. Incrementally innovative: This type of *kaikaku* is common when there are new production management tools or solutions introduced to the company. It is said to be incremental because the new production system is not actually new. It is only new to the company but has been used by other companies in similar industries.
   b. Radically innovative: This *kaikaku* makes the company unique in the industry. It is said to be radical because the production system introduced to the company is not only new but also new to the industry.

2. Implementation includes infrastructure and structural aspects.
   a. Infrastructure: Infrastructure change, for instance, occurs in production control system, material flow, quality control system, and organization. Changes in infrastructural aspect require active involvement of the employees and consistency in the improvement behavior pattern. Major changes occur through the cumulative effect of sustained efforts. Therefore, infrastructural change requires continuous and consistent efforts to improve operation. Change at infrastructural level is soft-oriented in the sense of involving basic changes in working ways. Included in the infrastructure are
      • Human resources, such as payment system, evaluation system, relationship with trade unions
      • Production planning and control, such as inventory, ordering system, and batch size
      • Quality control, for instance, defect prevention and supervision
      • Cost control, such as cost calculation and accounting
      • Material flow, such as connectivity and layout
      • Care, such as routine and supervision
      • Organization, includes structure and culture

b. Structure. Changes in structural aspect tend to require large capital investments. In addition, it is difficult to undo or cancel changes if they occur. Therefore, structural changes have a long-term impact. There are four types of structural aspects in the company, namely:
- Production capacity, such as volume per year
- Factory network design, such as size, location, and focus
- Production technology, such as equipment and autonomy level
- Vertical integration, both in terms of direction and area

From these two dimensions there are four combinations characterizing *kaikaku* (Yamamoto, 2010):

1. Structural changes: This is *kaikaku* type I. The examples of structural changes are replacement with new available production equipment in the industry or increasing automation level in equipment outside the rack. Structural changes are incremental innovation conducted in the structural aspect. This type of change can occur by importing existing solutions in the structural aspect.
2. Infrastructure changes: This is *kaikaku* type II. The example is importing a set of work processes developed by outsiders or introducing available work methods such as TPM (Total Productive Maintenance), Six Sigma, and lean. Infrastructure changes are incremental innovation conducted in infrastructure sector.
3. Structural changes exceed normal condition. This is *kaikaku* type III. The example is finding new production equipment and used in the company. Toyota, introduced a number of innovative equipment in its factory in Takaoka. Structural changes exceed normal condition is radical innovation in the structural aspect. In this *kaikaku*, new technology, new production equipment, or other solutions related to the structural aspect are found and applied on factories or companies.
4. Infrastructure changes exceed normal condition. This is *kaikaku* type IV. The example is finding new working methods and used in companies. This can be seen in the case of Ricoh United which succeeded in aligning the length of assembly line with the production volume using interconnected trolleys drawn with an electric motor as a substitute for ordinary conveyor lines. This step results in a reduction of waiting time and inventory in process up to 80%. Infrastructure changes beyond normal condition are the result of radical innovation in infrastructure sector.

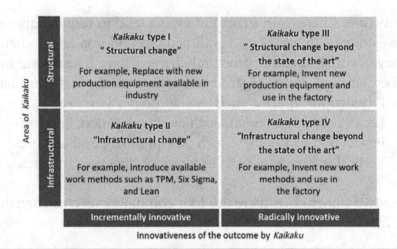

Figure 15.2 *Kaikaku* **classification (Yamamoto, 2010).**

Figure 15.2 indicates the changes in position in kaikaku classification system.

Kaizen

Kaizen implies incremental changes. It is different from *kaikaku, kaizen* works continuously because it implies only small changes (Scherger, 2003). *Kaizen* is directed in workflow to improve the continuous improvement cycle and prepare the way for lean principles in the next cycle. *Kaizen* does not change the production's basic model.

Kaizen runs at a short and fast time, referred to as *kaizen* event. Nissan, for example, in 1977 used two days of *kaizen*, which meant making incremental changes that must be resolved in two days (Montabon, 2005). Montabon (2005) provides an example of *kaizen* events in general by taking three days as follows:

1. Day 1
    a. Events begin with the inauguration, include talks from the person who submitted the idea for the event and/or who sponsored the event.
    b. Training short period, where *kaizen* event process is explained.
    c. Current process is mapped.
    d. Benchmark process is made if there is available data.
    e. At the end of the day, brainstorm new ideas.

2. Day 2
    a. Brainstorming continued, but most of day 2 is used to try new ideas.
    b. Implementation plans are withdrawn if it is needed for worth adopting ideas.
3. Day 3
    a. Completion of not-conducted experiment, but most of day 3 is used to implement the solutions from the team.
    b. In case where the solution definitely requires a longer implementation period, finalize the plans for achieving implementation.
    c. The team also prepares a solution presentation, which will be given to top management to complete the event.
    d. In addition, there is usually a dinner to thank for the long and intensive work done during the three days (or more).

Success of a lean event depends on many factors. Farris, Van Aken, Doolen, and Worley (2009) have collected various factors to support the success of *kaizen* events:

1. 5S
2. Sharing knowledge
3. Culture supporting changes
4. List of action items
5. Historical performances data
6. Management support, including top management and work area managers
7. Short/limited duration
8. Flexibility approach
9. Narrow focus
10. Team functional heterogeneity
11. Rewards for participation
12. Low capital investment
13. Job safety
14. Purpose clarity
15. Ability to justify events financially
16. Difficulties of purpose
17. Employee involvement and work area management in *kaizen* events
18. Resource availability
19. Expectation beliefs and assignment values

20. Problem complexity
21. Consistency focusing on improvement
22. Full-time *kaizen* event coordinator
23. Quality of *kaizen* program champion (sponsor), communication, and team leader
24. Action-oriented
25. Team autonomy
26. Training, mainly in new work methods
27. Use specific and legitimate metrics
28. Employee empowerment
29. Recognition of change
30. Facilitators and team leaders experience
31. Tools and team process knowledge
32. Performance measurement
33. Repetition
34. Measurement system adjustment and strategic adjustment
35. Achievement behavior
36. Standard operating procedure
37. Effective internal process
38. Team functional representation
39. Follow-up review
40. Scope of events
41. Team-based nature
42. Problem-solving system
43. Organizational stability
44. Survey of employee needs
45. Without manipulation or competition
46. Employee turnover
47. Time to complete the action items

Further, Farris et al. (2009) identified two types of outcomes produced by *kaizen* events, namely, social system outcome and technical system outcome:

1. Social system outcome, that is HR impact of lean, includes
    a. *Kaizen* capability. This includes team members' knowledge improvement on continuous improvement and problem-solving skills enhancement, including

- Knowledge improvement of what continuous improvement is
- Knowledge improvement of how continuous improvement is conducted
- Knowledge improvement of team members on the needs to create continuous improvements
- Knowledge improvement of team members' role in continuous improvement
- Ability to communicate new ideas on improvement as a result of *kaizen* event participation
- New skills as a result of *kaizen* event participation
- Team members' motivation to perform better
- Increase in team members' interest in their work
- Help people in the relevant field to work together and improve performance

b. Attitude is the impact on the motivation of team members. Attitude is seen from:

- Willingness to be a part of *kaizen* event
- Desire to be a part of next *kaizen* event in the future
- Convenience in working with other people to identify improvements in their working area

2. Technical system output, that is the impact of events on technical performance of target working area, including

a. Target achievement

b. Impact on working field

c. Overall success perception

References

Achanga, P., Shehab, E., Roy, R., & Nelder, G. (2006). Critical success factors for lean implementation within SMEs. Journal of Manufacturing Technology Management, 17(4), 460–471. https://doi.org/10.1108/17410380610662889

Adler, N., Hakkert, A. S., Kornbluth, J., & Hakkert, A. S. (2012). Lean management for Traffic-Police Enforcement Planning. Policing: An International Journal of Police Strategies & Management, 35(4), 662–686. https://doi.org/10.1108/13639511211275382

Adnan, A. N. Bin, Jaffar, A. Bin, Yusoff, N. B., & Halim, N. H. B. A. (2013). Implementation of Just in Time Production through Kanban System. Industrial Engineering Letters, 3(6), 11–20. Retrieved from http://www.iiste.org/Journals/index.php/IEL/article/view/6228%5Cnhttp://www.iiste.org/Journals/index.php/IEL/article/download/6228/6357

Afrin, A. B., & Islam, R. (2018). A Conceptual Model of Continuous Improvement in Total Quality Management from Islamic Perspective. Australian Academy of Business and Economics Review (AABER), 4(1), 1–16.

Alizon, F., Shooter, S. B., & Simpson, T. W. (2009). Henry Ford and the Model T: lessons for product platforming and mass customization. Design Studies, 30(5), 588–605. https://doi.org/10.1016/j.destud.2009.03.003

Alves, A. C., Dinis-Carvalho, J., Sousa, R. M., Moreira, F., & Lima, R. M. (2011). Benefits of Lean Management: Results form some Industrial Cases in Portugal. In 6° Congresso Luso-Moçambicano de Engenharia (CLME'2011).

Anderson-Connolly, R., Grunberg, L., Greenberg, E. S., & Moore, S. (2002). Is lean mean? Workplace transformation and employee well-being. Work, Employment and Society, 16(3), 389–413. https://doi.org/10.1177/095001702762217407

Andersson, R., Eriksson, H., & Torstensson, H. (2006). Similarities and differences between TQM, six sigma and lean. The TQM Magazine, 18(3), 282–296. https://doi.org/10.1108/09544780610660004

Antony, J. (2011). Six Sigma vs Lean. International Journal of Productivity and Performance Management, 60(2), 185–190. https://doi.org/10.1108/17410401111101494

Arnheiter, E. D., & Maleyeff, J. (2005). The integration of lean management and Six Sigma. The TQM Magazine, 17(1), 5–18. https://doi.org/10.1108/09544780510573020

Aslanzadeh, Y., & Davoodi, A. (2014). Stage-Gate modified for Lean PD. Chalmers University of Technology.

Bame, C. A. (2017). Application of Lean Manufacturing Principles to the Healthcare Workforce Training System: Using lean principles to determine best practices in healthcare workforce planning for Linn, Benton, and Lincoln Counties (Oregon). Oregon State University.

Bay, B. K., Tang, N. K. H., & Bennett, D. (2004). An empirical study of the imperatives for a supply chain implementation project in Seagate Technology International. Supply Chain Management: An International Journal, 9(4), 331–340. https://doi.org/10.1108/13598540410550082

Bhasin, S., & Burcher, P. (2006). Lean viewed as a philosophy. Journal of Manufacturing Technology Management, 17(1), 56–72. https://doi.org/10.1108/17410380610639506

Bhatia, N., & Drew, J. (2007). Applying Lean production to the public sector. The McKinsey Quarterly, 1–5. Retrieved from http://executivesondemand.net/managementsourcing/images/stories/artigos_pdf/produtividade/Applying_lean_production_to_the_public_sector.pdf

Biswas, R. (2013). Productivity Improvement in Garments Industry through Cellular Manufacturing Approach Productivity Improvement in Garments Industry Through Cellular Manufacturing. Bangladesh University of Engineering and Technology.

Boehm, B. (2005). The Future of Software and Systems Engineering Processes. Retrieved from http://sunset.usc.edu/csse/TECHRPTS/2005/usccse2005-507/usccse2005-507.pdf

Bozdogan, K., Milauskas, R., Mize, J., Nightingale, D., Taneja, A., & Tonaszuck, D. (2000). Transitioning to a lean enterprise: a guide for leaders (Vol. III). Retrieved from http://scholar.google.com/scholar?hl=en&btnG=Search&q=intitle:Transitioning+to+a+Lean+Enterprise:+A+Guide+for+Leaders#0%5Cnhttp://scholar.google.com/scholar?hl=en&btnG=Search&q=intitle:Transitioning+to+a+lean+enterprise:+a+guide+for+leaders%230

Cankovic, M., Varney, R. C., Whiteley, L., Brown, R., D'Angelo, R., Chitale, D., & Zarbo, R. J. (2009). The Henry Ford production system: LEAN process redesign improves service in the molecular diagnostic laboratory. Journal of Molecular Diagnostics, 11(5), 390–399. https://doi.org/10.2353/jmoldx.2009.090002

Childs, H. C. (2017). Strategies that Logistics Leaders use for Achieving Successful Process Improvement. Walden University.

Čiarnienė, R., & Vienažindienė, M. (2013). Lean Manufacturing Implementation: the Main Chalenges and Barriers. Management Theory and Studies for Rural Business and Infrastructure Development, 35(1), 41–48.

Construction Task Force. (1998). Rethinking Construction. London.

Crawford, C. a. (2006). Advanced Engineering Models for Wind Turbines with Application to the Design of a Coning Rotor Concept. University of Cambridge.

D'Angelo, R., & Zarbo, R. J. (2007). The Henry Ford production system: Measures of process defects and waste in surgical pathology as a basis for quality improvement initiatives. American Journal of Clinical Pathology, 128(3), 423–429. https://doi.org/10.1309/X6N1Y3V2CB9HUL8G

Damrath, F. (2012). Increasing competitiveness of service companies: developing conceptual models for implementing Lean Management in service companies, (June).

Demeter, K., & Matyusz, Z. (2011). The impact of lean practices on Inventory Turnover. International Journal of Production Economics, 133(1), 154–163. https://doi.org/10.1109/ICMIT.2016.7605006

Dentz, J., Nahmens, I., & Mullens, M. (2009). Applying Lean Production in Factory Homebuilding. Cityscape: A Journal of Policy Development and Research, 11(1), 81–104.

Drewery, K. (2003). Harnessing Creativity and Innovation.

Ehsanifar, F., & Rubin, J. L. R. (2011). Exploring Lean Principles in Automotive Aftermarket for Spare Parts Distribution: A Case Study at Volvo Parts. Chalmers University of Technology.

El Gohary, M. A. (2005). A Process for Reducing Preliminary Engineering Costs for Multi-Sided Steel Poles. Oklahoma State University.

El Shenawy, E., Baker, T., & Lemak, D. J. (2007). A meta-analysis of the effect of TQM on competitive advantage. International Journal of Quality & Reliability Management (Vol. 24). https://doi.org/10.1108/02656710710748349

Emiliani, M. L., & Stec, D. J. (2004). Using value-stream maps to improve leadership. Leadership & Organization Development Journal, 25(8), 622–645. https://doi.org/10.1108/01437730410564979

Farris, J. A., Van Aken, E. M., Doolen, T. L., & Worley, J. (2009). Critical success factors for human resource outcomes in Kaizen events: An empirical study. International Journal of Production Economics, 117(1), 42–65. https://doi.org/10.1016/j.ijpe.2008.08.051

Fillingham, D. (2007). Can lean save lives? Leadership in Health Services, 20(4), 231–241. https://doi.org/10.1108/17511870710829346

Flumerfelt, S., & Green, G. (2013). Using lean in the flipped classroom for at risk students. Educational Technology and Society, 16(1), 356–366. https://doi.org/http://www.jstor.org/stable/jeductechsoci.16.1.356?seq=1&cid=pdf-%0Areference#references_tab_contents

Frid, M., & Utterstrom, E. (2014). Lean into your processes The importance of getting to know your processes and the people involved.

Gabay, R. (2012). Deming' s 14 Principles. Quasar, 10–11.

George, M. L. (2003). Lean Six Sigma for Service. New York: McGraw-Hill.

Glazer, H., Dalton, J., Anderson, D., Konrad, M., & Shrum, S. (2008). CMMI ® or Agile: Why Not Embrace Both! https://doi.org/10.1109/AGILE.2006.30

Gorenflo, G., & Moran, J. W. (2010). The ABC's of PDCA. Public Health Foundation, (March), 56–60. https://doi.org/10.1097/01.ASW.0000363526.70383.c2

Gupta, M., & Campbell, V. S. (1995). The Cost of Quality. Production and Inventory Management Journal, 36(3), 43–49.

Haak, R. (2004). Changing Patters of Japanese Production Management–A new Balance between Tradition and Innovation. Euij.Sakura.Ne.Jp, (November), 1–27. Retrieved from http://euij.sakura.ne.jp/pub/research_papers/20041126_Workshop/Workshop-2004-11-26-Haak.pdf

Haak, R. (2006). Implementing Process Innovation – The Case of the Toyota Production System. In C. Herstatt, C. Stockstrom, H. Tschirky, & A. Nagahira (Eds.), Management of Technology and Innovation in Japan (pp. 185–207). Hamburg: Springer. https://doi.org/10.1007/3-540-31248–X

Hallam, C. R.., Muesel, J., & W. Flannery. (2010). Analysis of the Toyota Production System and the Genesis of Six Sigma Programs: An Imperative for Understanding Failures in Technology Management Culture Transformation in Traditional Manufacturing Companies. Technology Management for Global Economic Growth (PICMET), 2010 Proceedings of PICMET '10:, 1–11.

Hardon, J., Montecinos, C., & Roberts, T. (2005). ETC Group External Review Report.

Hasani, T., Bojei, J., & Dehghantanha, A. (2017). Investigating the antecedents to the adoption of SCRM technologies by start up companies. Telematics and Informatics, 34(5), 655–675.

Hines, P., Holweg, M., Rich, N., Hines, P., Holweg, M., & Rich, N. (2006). Learning to evolve A review of contemporary lean thinking. https://doi.org/10.1108/01443570410558049

Höök, M. (2008). Lean Culture in Industrialized Housing - a study of Timber Volume Element Prefabrication.

Hopp, W. J., & Spearman, M. L. (2004). To Pull or Not to Pull: What Is the Question? Manufacturing & Service Operations Management, 6(2), 133–148. https://doi.org/10.1287/msom.1030.0028

Hult, G. T. M. (2011). Toward a theory of the boundary-spanning marketing organization and insights from 31 organization theories. Journal of Academy of Marketing Science, 39, 509–536. https://doi.org/10.1007/s11747-011-0253–6.

Humphreys, K. K. (2011). Toyota Production System. Toyota Production System. Productivity Press. https://doi.org/10.1201/b11731.

Jansson, G., Soderholm, E., & Johnsson, H. (2009). Design Process Organisation at Industrial House Builders. Lulea University of Technology.

Julien, A. S. (2011). Mapping the inbound logistics of the refineries & terminals (plants) onshore at StatoilHydro, identify main problems and issues and suggest quick wins and possible solutions. University of Stavanger.

Juran, J. M. (1986). The quality trilogy: A universal approach to managing for quality. Quality Progress.

Kang, K., & Apte, U. (2007). Lean Six Sigma Implementation for Military Logistics to Improve Readiness. In 4th Annual Acquisition Research Symposium of the Naval Postgraduate School (pp. 599–614).

Keif, M. (2006, November). Why Aren't We Leaner in the United States? Flexo, 24–26.

Kilpatrick, J. (2003). Lean Principles. Utah Manufacturing Extension Partnership, 1–5.

Kim, C. S., Spahlinger, D. A., Kin, J. M., & Billi, J. E. (2006). Lean health care: what can hospitals learn from a world-class automaker? Journal of Hospital Medicine (Online), 1(3), 191–199. https://doi.org/10.1002/jhm.68

Kinnie, N., Hutchinson, S., & Purcell, J. (1998). Downsizing: is it always lean and mean? Personnel Review, 27(4), 296–311. https://doi.org/10.1108/00483489810213883

Lempia, D. (2008). Using lean principles and MBE in design and development of avionics equipment at rockwell collins. In ICAS Secretariat -26th Congress of International Council of the Aeronautical Sciences 2008, ICAS 2008 (Vol. 1, pp. 3905–3918). Retrieved from http://www.scopus.com/inward/record.url?eid=2-s2.0-84878927269&partnerID=tZOtx3y1

Lian, C. P. (2006). Production Operation System – Key Performance Indicator. University of Southern Queensland.

Liberopoulos, G., & Dallery, Y. (2002). Base stock versus WIP cap in single-stage make-to-stock production-inventory systems. IIE Transactions (Institute of Industrial Engineers), 34(7), 627–636. https://doi.org/10.1080/07408170208928899

Liker, J. K., & Morgan, J. M. (2006). The Toyota Way in Services: The Case of Lean Product Development. Academy of Management Perspectives, 20(2), 5–20. https://doi.org/10.5465/AMP.2006.20591002

Lim, C. H. D. (2009). Building a Customer Centric Business for Service Excellence and Competitive Advantage in the Singapore Banking Industry. The University of Nottingham.

Lindhard, S., & Wandahl, S. (2012). The robust schedule - A link to improved workflow. In Proceedings for IGLC 20. International Group for Lean Construction. Retrieved from http://www.scopus.com/inward/record.url?eid=2-s2.0-84874490110&partnerID=tZOtx3y1

Manzouri, M., Ab-Rahman, M. N., Zain, C. R. C. M., & Jamsari, E. A. (2014). Increasing production and eliminating waste through lean tools and techniques for Halal food companies. Sustainability, 6(12), 9179–9204. https://doi.org/10.3390/su6129179

Martichenko, R., & Taylor, L. (2006). Lean Transportation: Fact or Fiction? FedEx White Paper, 1–9.

Middleton, P., Flaxel, A., & Cookson, A. (2005). Lean Software Management Case Study: Timberline Inc. In H. Baumeister, M. Marchesi, & M. Holcombe (Eds.), Lecture Notes in Computer Science 3556 (pp. 1–9). Berlin: Springer. https://doi.org/10.1007/b137278

Millman, T., Wilson, K., Stevensen, C., & Cooper, N. (1995). From key account selling to key account management. : : Qualitative and Quantitative Research, 57(6), 9–21. https://doi.org/10.2501/IJMR–2015–070

Montabon, F. (2005). Using kaizen events for back office processes: The recruitment of frontline supervisor co-ops. Total Quality Management and Business Excellence, 16(10), 1139–1147. https://doi.org/10.1080/14783360500235876

Monteiro, M., Pacheco, C., Dinis-Carvalho, J., & Paiva, F. (2015). Implementing lean office: A successful case in public sector. FME Transaction, 43(4), 303–310. https://doi.org/10.5937/fmet1504303M

Moodaliyar, R. (2010). The Effectiveness of the ISO 9001:2000 Quality Management Standard on Performance and Customer Satisfaction at a Selected Organisation. Durban University of Technology.

Morgan, J., & Company, F. M. (2011). Lean Product Development as a System: A Case Study of Body and Stamping Development at Ford, 23(1).

Murman, E. (2003). Lean Systems Engineering II.

Nahmens, I., & Ikuma, L. H. (2012). Effects of Lean Construction on Sustainability of Modular Homebuilding, (June), 155–163. https://doi.org/10.1061/(ASCE) AE.1943-5568.0000054.

Nakayama, S., & Mgbike, U. (2010). Risk Assessment: A Proactive Approach to Minimizing Waste.

Näslund, D. (2008). Lean, six sigma and lean sigma: fads or real process improvement methods? Business Process Management Journal, 14(3), 269–287. https://doi.org/10.1108/14637150810876634

Norberg, H. (2008). on-Site Production Synchronisation. Lulea University of Technology.

Oakland, J. S. (2003). Statistical Process Control. Oxford: Butterworth Heinemann. https://doi.org/10.1016/B978-075066529-2/50008-5

Oh, H. (1999). Service quality, customer satisfaction, and customer value: A holistic perspective. Hospitality Management, 18, 67–82. https://doi.org/10.1016/S0278-4319(98)00047-4

Papadopoulou, T. C. (2013). Application of lean scheduling and production control in non-repetitive manufacturing systems using intelligent agent decision support. Brunel University.

Parnell-Klabo, E. (2006). Introducing lean principles with Agile practices at a fortune 500 company. In Proceedings - AGILE Conference, 2006 (pp. 232–239). https://doi.org/10.1109/AGILE.2006.35

Patel, C., & Ramachandran, M. (2009). Story card Maturity Model (SMM): A process improvement framework for agile requirements engineering practices. Journal of Software, 4(5), 422–435. https://doi.org/10.4304/jsw.4.5.422-435

Petersen, K., & Wohlin, C. (2009). Measuring the flow in lean software development. Software Practice and Experience, 41(00), 1–7. https://doi.org/10.1002/spe

Radnor, Z., & Walley, P. (2008). Learning to walk before we try to run: Adapting lean for the public sector. Public Money and Management, 28(1), 13–20. https://doi.org/10.1111/j.1467-9302.2008.00613.x

Ramadan, M. A. (2015). The effectiveness of strategic Human Resources Management (HRM) on developing the Lean-Centric Approach (LCA) towards Integrated Supply Chain Management (ISCM) sustainability. International Journal of Advance Research in Computer Science and Management Studies, 3(11), 337–350.

Ray, B., Ripley, P., & Neal, D. (2006). Lean Manufacturing: A Systematic Approach to Improving Productivity in the Precast Concrete Industry. Precast-Prestressed Concrete Institute Journal, 62–71.

Reich, A. Z., Mccleary, K. W., & Hall, W. (2006). The Roles of Product and Service Quality in Determining Brand Loyalty: An exploratory investigation of quick service restaurants.

Robinson, S., Radnor, Z. J., Burgess, N., & Worthington, C. (2012). SimLean: Utilizing Simulation in the Implementation of Lean in Healthcare. European Journal of Operational Research, 219(1), 188–197.

Roh, J., Hong, P., & Min, H. (2014). Implementation of a responsive supply chain strategy in global complexity: The case of manufacturing firms. International Journal of Production Economics, 147(PART B), 198–210. https://doi.org/10.1016/j.ijpe.2013.04.013

Russo-spena, T., & Mele, C. (n.d.). Tiziana Russo-Spena and Cristina Mele.

Sacks, R., Radosavljevic, M., & Barak, R. (2010). Requirements for building information modeling based lean production management systems for construction. Automation in Construction, 19(5), 641–655. https://doi.org/10.1016/j.autcon.2010.02.010

Salman, D. A. (2017). Lean Thinking and its Role in the Development of Value - Oriented Product. Bingol University.

Scherger, J. E. (2005). The end of the beginning: The redesign imperative in family medicine. Family Medicine, 37(7), 513–516.

Schiffauerova, A., & Thomson, V. (2006). A review of research on cost of quality models and best practices. International Journal of Quality & Reliability Management, 23(6), 647–669. https://doi.org/http://dx.doi.org/10.1108/09564230910978511

Setia, P., Venkatesh, V., & Joglekar, S. (2013). Leveraging Digital Technologies: How Information Quality Leads to Localized Capabilities and Customer Service Performance. MIS Quarterly, 37(2), 565–590.

Shah, R., & Ward, P. T. (2007). Defining and developing measures of lean production. Journal of Operations Management, 25(4), 785–805. https://doi.org/10.1016/j.jom.2007.01.019

Shamah, R. A. M. (2013). Measuring and building lean thinking for value creation in supply chains. International Journal of Lean Six Sigma, 4(1), 17–35. https://doi.org/10.1108/20401461311310490

Shang, G., & Pheng, L. S. (2014). Barriers to lean implementation in the construction industry in China. Journal of Technology Management in China, 9(2), 155–173. https://doi.org/10.1108/JTMC-12-2013-0043

Spear, S., & Bowen, H. K. (1999). Decoding the DNA of the Toyota Production System. Harvard Business Review, 77(5), 96–106. https://doi.org/http://search.ebscohost.com/login.aspx?direct=true&db=buh&AN=2216294&site=ehost-live

Staats, B. R., James, D., & Upton, D. M. (2011). Lean principles, learning, and knowledge work: Evidence from a software services provider. Journal of Operations Management, 29(5), 376–390. https://doi.org/10.1016/j.jom.2010.11.005

Sunder, V. M. (2013). Synergies of Lean Six Sigma. IUP Journal of Operations Management, 12, 21–31. Retrieved from http://papers.ssrn.com/sol3/papers.cfm?abstract_id=2255845

Taylor, S., & Lyon, P. (1995). Paradigm lost: the rise and fall of McDonaldization. International Journal of Contemporary Hospitality Management, 7(2/3), 64–68. https://doi.org/10.1108/09596119510080024

Teece, D., & Pisano, G. (2004). The Dynamic Capabilities of Firms. In Handbook on Knowledge Management (Vol. 3, pp. 195–213). https://doi.org/10.1093/icc/3.3.537–a

Timans, W., Antony, J., Ahaus, K., & Van Solingen, R. (2012). Implementation of Lean Six Sigma in small- and medium-sized manufacturing enterprises in the Netherlands. Journal of the Operational Research Society, 63(3), 339–353. https://doi.org/10.1057/jors.2011.47

Tommelein, I. D. (1998). Pull-Driven Scheduling for Pipe-Spool Installation: Simulation of a Lean Construction Technique. ASCE Journal of Construction Engineering and Management, 124(4), 279–288.

Tyagi, R. K., Varma, N., & Vidyarthi, N. (2013). An Integrated Framework for Service Quality: SQBOK Perspective. QMJ, 20(2), 34–48.

Verhoef, P. C., & Leeflang, P. S.. (2009). Understanding the Marketing Department's Influence Within the Firm. Journal of Marketing, 73(2), 14–37. https://doi.org/10.1509/jmkg.73.2.14

Vessell, A. L. (2006). Optimizing the Sequenced Production Schedule by Managing the Internal Supply Chain. Massachusetts Institute of Technology.

Wang, L., Ming, X. G., Kong, F. B., Li, D., & Wang, P. P. (2011). Focus on implementation: a framework for lean product development. Journal of Manufacturing Technology Management, 23(1), 4–24. https://doi.org/10.1108/17410381211196267

Wanjiku, N. R. (2010). Managing growth in small and medium enterprises among members of the nairobi stock exchange: A case of Suntra investment bank. University of Nairobi.

Whiting, H. S., & Weckman, G. R. (2004). Reducing Cycle Time for a Restaurant Drive - Thru Simulation. In IIE Annual Conference Proceedings. Retrieved from https://www.researchgate.net/profile/Gary_Weckman/publication/263313007_Reducing_Cycle_Time_for_a_Restaurant_Drive-Thru_Simulation/links/5525cc140cf295bf160eb345/Reducing-Cycle-Time-for-a-Restaurant-Drive-Thru-Simulation.pdf

Wojtys, E. M., Schley, L., Overgaard, K. A., & Agbabian, J. (2009). Applying Lean Techniques to Improve the Patient Scheduling Process. Journal for Healthcare Quality, 31(3), 10–16.

Yamamoto, Y. (2010). Kaikaku in production. Malardalen University. Retrieved from http://mdh.diva-portal.org/smash/record.jsf?pid=diva2%3A319289&dswid=8502

Yang, M., Hong, P., & Modi, S. B. (2011). Impact of lean manufacturing and environmental management on business performance: An empirical study of manufacturing firms. Intern. Journal of Production Economics, 129, 251–261. https://doi.org/10.1016/j.ijpe.2010.10.017

Zarbo, R. J. (2012). Creating and sustaining a lean culture of continuous process improvement. American Journal of Clinical Pathology, 138(3), 321–326. https://doi.org/10.1309/AJCP2QY1XGKTSNQF

Index